# Unlocking Horns

**FORGIVENESS AND
RECONCILIATION
IN BURUNDI**

By David Niyonzima
and Lon Fendall

BARCLAY PRESS

Newberg, Oregon

# Unlocking Horns

## FORGIVENESS AND RECONCILIATION
## IN BURUNDI

International Standard Book Number: 0-913342-97-1

Library of Congress Control Number: 2001095459

Cover design and page layout by Michael Comfort

Drawings on cover and inside pages by Debbie Ellingsworth

# TABLE OF CONTENTS

## THE AUTHORS

David Niyonzima is superintendent (legal representative) of Burundi Yearly Meeting of Friends. He is currently working on a graduate degree in counseling at George Fox University in Newberg, Oregon. David received his bachelor's degree from Kenya Highlands Bible College.

Lon Fendall is dean of undergraduate studies at George Fox University. He is chair of the advisory committee of the Great Lakes School of Theology, in Bujumbura, Burundi. This book project is part of his work with Good News Associates.

## THE ILLUSTRATOR

Debbie Ellingsworth is on the staff of the Murdock Learning Resource Center of George Fox University. Along with her interest in art, she has been involved with drama ministries with Wycliffe Bible Translators.

# FOREWORD

In the Psalms, the poet sings:

*Since my youth, O God, you have taught me,*

*and to this day I declare your marvelous deeds.*

*Even when I am old and gray,*

*do not forsake me, O God,*

*till I declare your power to the next generation,*

*your might to all who are to come.*

—Psalm 71:17-18

Fortunately, David Niyonzima and Lon Fendall have not waited until they are "old and gray" to record their story about God's deeds, power, and might at work in Burundi. This generation, and the next, needs to hear their story. Both authors have learned from God in their respective but distant homes; David, the son of a Quaker leader in Burundi; and Lon, the son of Quaker farmers in Oregon. David heard of America through the missionaries who lived near his home at Kwibuka mission station. Lon learned of Burundi through the same missionaries who hosted his visit during his graduate studies. They both absorbed the Quaker teaching that God's love transcends boundaries of nation, race, and group identity and that

He intends for humankind to live at peace and to establish justice for the poor and afflicted. Now both authors have been drawn into the complexities of the chaos and violence in Central Africa. David has suffered tragic loss and displacement on both sides of his family. Lon, who first visited Burundi in 1965, carrying forward a long tradition of Quaker concern for that area, has more recently been engaged in reconciliation initiatives there.

In this book, these Quaker scholars grapple with the challenges that God's plan of peace and the good news of reconciliation pose to the violence and chaos of central Africa. That challenge defies logic and experience. Where in Central Africa, clouded with incredible inhumanity among humans, are the marvelous deeds, power, and might of God? Niyonzima and Fendall offer some illuminating answers. God in His power chose to endue the people of this region with a sense of His greatness and love (see Romans 1:18-19). In spite of their worship of spirits (imandwa), the people of Burundi and other kingdoms in this region traditionally knew of Imana, the Creator God who loved His people. God in His might gave the traditional society norms of justice and canons for coexistence, which despite hierarchies and clans, bound together a diverse people into one nation. The peoples of Central Africa were culturally prepared to receive a message of reconciliation and peace.

God's marvelous deeds included stirring up missionaries to come to Central Africa with the Gospel: first Catholic White Fathers, then German Lutherans, and then, in the region where David grew up, the Quakers. Although initially resisted, Christianity in two generations became the faith of most people. God in His power quickened the hearts of new converts in the late twenties and thirties with a revival spirit that broke down barriers of race, clan and custom. God in His might built His church with a wide ministry in education and health care and an extraordinary atmosphere of collaboration and unity among evangelical missions as varied as Baptists and Anglicans.

But pride and passion have also been at work in Central Africa. The colonial state, built on the authority structures of traditional monarchies in Rwanda and Burundi gave way to independent and (on paper) constitutional governments. But, with the coming of independence, the competition for power and its economic benefits justified itself in ethnic terms and adopted violence and intimidation as an appropriate methodology. In Burundi, in addition to the assassinations of two prime ministers and the near death of a third, political pogroms broke out in 1965, 1969, 1972, 1988, and 1993.

The country is today racked by rebellion and internal political struggles. Most foreign missionaries, suspected of supporting one side or the other, were eventually sent home. Yet, against all that man could do to unleash the forces of violence and evil, God in His might has comforted His people in their sorrow and anguish, energized a new revival in His church, and raised in its leaders a consciousness of the church's ministry of reconciliation, "Unlocking Horns."

This valued and fascinating history is largely told in traditional style as a fireside dialogue with a curious young friend, Emmanuel. But the book is also an instruction in righteousness. Out of the crucible of conflict in Burundi, Niyonzima and Fendall draw the lesson that favoritism undermines faith, that deference to wealth and status leads to despising the poor and afflicted, and that hateful words lead to hateful actions. They find the biblical remedy to these problems by reconnecting faith to loving action and nurturing the culture of peace. Not a theoretical homily, this book details some practical initiatives to bringing reconciliation to Burundi and offers individuals stories of God's grace and deliverance in the midst of suffering.

Lon Fendall and David Niyonzima have recounted David's personal experience in the context of the cultural changes and political complexities that confront Burundi today. The book was written in the hope that, once translated into Kirundi—a language familiar to some 20 million people around Central Africa's great lakes—it would provide insight into the past and fresh hope that living out the love of Christ can help break the cycle of violence and revenge. Those outside Central Africa who read the story can better understand one of the most tragic conflicts of our time. Those who share the authors' hope in Christ's peace can better pray for Burundi, Rwanda, and Congo in the manner that Jews were instructed to pray for Jerusalem, that there may "be peace within your walls and security within your citadels." (Psalm 122:7)

—David P. Rawson
*Former U.S. ambassador to Rwanda*

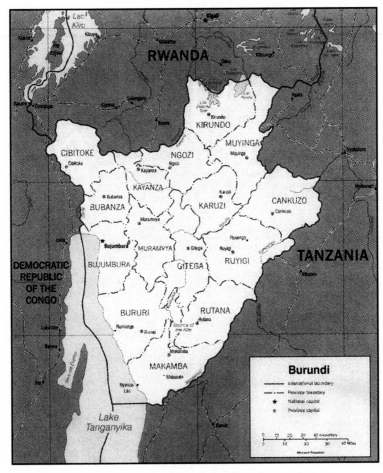

Courtesy of *The General Libraries, The University of Texas at Austin*

# PREFACE

## FROM DAVID NIYONZIMA:

There is much that is discouraging about the recent history of Burundi. Just in the last decade hundreds of thousands of people have been killed and many more have fled the country. Looking back at the seventies, when the first major bloodshed occurred, there were hundreds of thousands of others who lost their lives, who fled the country, or who were displaced within the country.

The international community has been at a loss to know what to do about violence in Burundi. Some mediation efforts have been under way in recent months, most notably involving Nelson Mandela of South Africa. Economic aid has been given in considerable amounts. But the fighting continues and economic conditions have worsened. More than half of my people live below the poverty line. Only about half the children are in school. Two-thirds of the people are illiterate. The infant mortality rate is 136 per 1,000. One in five Burundians are believed to be infected with HIV/AIDS. When adults die, invariably children are left as orphans. International workers have created a euphemism to apply to these children, calling them "unaccompanied children." Polite expressions cannot hide the terrible suffering of our people.

One of the tragedies of the human suffering in Burundi is that we have been blessed with a beautiful country. Some parts of Africa are so barren and dry that human survival is barely possible. But ours is a country blessed with good soil, abundant water, and a favorable climate. Early European explorers called it the "Switzerland of Africa." We have the physical means for our people to prosper. The one thing that bars the way to a happier future is the inability of our people to forgive one another for the hurts of the past and to trust one another to live at peace in the future. In many ways the situation seems hopeless. But we serve a God of miracles. Many people in South Africa in the last decade were discouraged about peace and justice being accomplished. But there were those who prayed and worked with all their energy for reconciliation, and we have seen much progress. If this came about in one of the worst cases of human hatred and mutual distrust, can it not come about for my country?

I have written this book to show the way from despair to hope. I am writing this for my own people, the people of Burundi. I also hope that the people of Rwanda, who have experienced a parallel but different history, will gain some insights and see the way past hatred to God's love. We share a similar language and much of the same history. Our two countries have influenced each other toward violence and now must help each other extract ourselves from an unending cycle of violence. Finally, I have written the book for people around the world who have struggled to understand the events in Burundi. As I have traveled in England and the United States, people have asked me to tell more of my story and to shed some light on similar problems elsewhere and I am pleased to be able to do this.

One of the legacies of the violence and suffering in Burundi during my lifetime is a spirit of hatred and distrust. We are so used to distrusting one another that we assume that each person sees the events of these decades from the limited perspective of their own ethnic group. I wish I could simply write as a Burundian, not as a Hutu, which happens to be the ethnic group into which I was born. I wish my wife, Felicity, could be seen as the wonderful and talented person she is, not primarily as a Tutsi. I wish the third ethnic group in Burundi, the Twa, weren't drawn into the struggles between the two larger groups and weren't seen as inferior to the other two. We can't change our ethnic background. But we can seek to understand better what it means to be one in the sight of God. And we can seek to live out the teaching of Galatians 3:28: "There is neither Jew nor Greek, slave nor free, male nor female, for you are all one in Christ Jesus."

As close as I have been to the problems of Burundi all my life, I confess that I don't always understand the enormous capacity of people to hate and fear each other. It's shocking and unbelievable that people will brutally kill one another and will continue to do that month after month, year after year. We Burundians, most of whom are Christian in some sense of the word, need to turn back to our Bible and find the explanation for the violence that is such a blight on Central Africa. One of the best biblical teachings on the transformation of human evil into superhuman love is the passage found in James 3:13-18:

*Who is wise and understanding among you? Let him show it by his good life, by deeds done in the humility that comes from wisdom. But if you harbor bitter envy and selfish ambition in your hearts, do not boast about it or deny the truth. Such "wisdom" does not come down from heaven but is earthly, unspiritual, of the devil. For where you have envy and selfish ambition, there you find disorder and every evil practice. But the wisdom that comes from heaven is first of all pure; then peace-loving, considerate, submissive, full of mercy and good fruit, impartial and sincere. Peacemakers who sow in peace raise a harvest of righteousness.*

I will say more about this passage in chapter eight.

This book is something that has been on my heart for a long time. I have searched for a way to help others see that Christians in Burundi have a great opportunity and responsibility to be peacemakers. In 1998 I wrote a small book, *"Indirimbo Ico Ari Co,"* about the role of music in healing the hurts of our land. As I was writing, I felt that God was telling me to write something more to help bring new hope to my people. I also wanted to do it in a way that would raise the awareness of people outside Burundi to the realities of my country. When Lon Fendall approached me about the possibility of working together on this book, I quickly realized that this was an answer to my prayer. Because of his expertise, wisdom, encouragement, and support, this dream has come true.

It was amazing when I came to George Fox University how everything seemed to contribute positively to the accomplishment of this project. Along with the assistance that I got from those who facilitated my enrollment, Roger and Mildred Minthorne invited me to stay in their home, providing for my needs and making me very comfortable. Ron Mock, director of the Center for Peace Learning at George Fox University, invited me to speak in his classes. The time I spent preparing for those classes helped me focus on what I would want to share in this book. The professors in the Department of Counseling also helped me explore the connection between personal healing and national peace building. While working on this book, I have also been able to finish the Kirundi translation of a training course called "Core Caring." The course was developed by Randy Michael, associate professor of marriage and family therapy at George Fox University. As this book was being finished, I was delighted to host Dr. Michael and a group of George Fox University students as they came to Burundi to teach a short course on healing from trauma.

In many of the chapters of the book, my thoughts take the form of a dialogue with a young friend of mine in Burundi, Emmanuel Ndikumana. He has been a good friend and I have been able to be his mentor from time to time. It is my hope that the stories I have shared with Emmanuel in this book will help the reader understand some of the complexities of the history and culture of Burundi.

## FROM LON FENDALL:

It was early June 1965 when I first visited Burundi. David Niyonzima was only six years old at the time. There would have been no reason for us to meet then, though it's possible I met his father. Burundi was the first major stop on my way home after spending a year as a graduate student at the University of Ghana. That adventure had begun during my junior year at George Fox College when one of the administrators said to me, "Our local Rotary Club is looking for someone to sponsor for the Rotary International graduate scholarship program. I'd like to recommend you for this program. Are you interested?" I couldn't have been more surprised and pleased. I had never been outside the United States, so studying for a year overseas sounded fascinating. I was fortunate enough to receive one of the scholarships and Rotary chose Ghana as my destination. At the time I knew very little about Ghana, one of the first African countries to gain its independence. I knew nothing about Kwame Nkrumah's presidency and about his leadership of African nationalism, socialism, and freedom from the control of the Western world.

I also knew very little about the University of Ghana before I arrived there in the fall of 1964. I had majored in religion and history at George Fox and thought I might take graduate courses at the University of Ghana in one or both of these fields. When I explored the possibilities after arriving, it was suggested I enroll in the Institute of African Studies. With no background in African studies whatsoever, I plunged into some fascinating and challenging seminars in African history, religion, literature, economics, and politics. The classes were wonderful and some included field trips within the country. There were some excellent scholars on the faculty at the institute and others came for visiting lectureships. I learned a lot about Africa, at least a great deal more than I knew before.

Flights across Africa were difficult to arrange in 1965 when it was time to leave Ghana, and it's still difficult. Even today, most flights come and go between Africa and Europe. But with the help of the Pan American Airways office in Accra, Ghana, I arranged a flight to Bujumbura, Burundi, via Lagos, Nigeria, and Leopoldville, Congo. I wanted to learn as much as I could about missions, especially the missions sponsored by the Friends Church. So I wrote to Friends missionaries in Africa and was able to spend a week in Burundi with Paul and Leona Thornburg, with James and Doris Morris, and others. I visited many other places before returning to Oregon, but that first stop was probably the most meaningful. I saw many churches and schools, the Radio CORDAC facility (which included a program to train Burundians in Christian radio), a print shop, medical clinics, a lepresarium, and other programs.

Burundi was beautiful and at the time peaceful, or so it seemed to me. True, there had been some political assassinations prior to my arrival, but there was not the kind of widespread, anti-European violence that had occurred in Kenya and elsewhere. But in October 1965, after I had left Burundi, the first widespread violence broke out.

I loved my year in Africa, especially the chance to study about Africa in some depth, but unfortunately I did not have a chance to visit Africa again until 1997. That year David Brandt, the president of Tabor College where I worked, suggested that my wife, Raelene, and I volunteer to go help at Daystar University in Nairobi, Kenya. He didn't need to twist our arms. Raelene had visited Kenya a few years before and had been on the campus of Daystar before it expanded to a new facility outside Nairobi. While we were there, Raelene assisted in the library and I taught a "summer block" course called "Peace and War in the Bible." Before going to Kenya, I had met David Niyonzima at a Quaker conference in the United States. I discovered that he was living in Kenya at the time, and I asked him if he would speak in my class at Daystar.

David gave my students a very helpful overview of the conflicts in Burundi from 1965 to 1997. The students, mostly from Kenya, appreciated David's lecture very much. Their comment was that except for God's grace, Kenya might be experiencing the kind of ethnic violence that had been going on in Burundi, Rwanda, and Congo. Raelene and I joined David for a worship service in Nairobi with other refugees from Burundi. We went with him to his home to meet his wife, Felicity, and their children, then went with them to enjoy a meal at a small outdoor restaurant. At the time David was doing what he could for reconciliation in Burundi from a distance, and it wasn't at all clear when it would be safe for him and his family to go back home.

Then in 1998, Ben Staley, missions chairman of Mid-America Friends Yearly Meeting, invited me to go to Burundi to help with plans for starting a Bible college. By then the Niyonzimas had been able to return to Burundi, where David could be more directly involved as legal representative (superintendent) of Burundi Friends Yearly Meeting. My part in this book came about from these contacts with David in 1997 and 1998. I heard him tell the story about the terrible death of his students at Kwibuka, which appears in chapter one. Then in early 2000, after another short visit to Kenya and Burundi, Raelene and I felt a call to return to Oregon and to make some time in our lives for writing and speaking. In the midst of exploring that call, I sent an e-mail to David, asking if it might be possible for us to work together on this project. His reply, dated April 17, 2000, was:

> I was very much thrilled by the idea of writing a book. I have longed to write a story about the ministry I have been involved in since I responded to the Lord's call. I could not figure out how this could be realized. I will be glad to work on it with you and provide you with whatever information you will judge necessary.

The amazing part of this dream of collaborating on a book was that while Raelene and I were feeling led to return to Oregon, David was seeking an opportunity to begin a graduate program in counseling. With the assistance of Ron Stansell, a Bible and missions professor at George Fox University, and David Brandt, president of George Fox (who had moved from Tabor College to George Fox University), David Niyonzima was able to enroll at George Fox in August 2000. So the two of us have been only a few miles apart as we have worked on this project. David spoke of being thrilled that this book has come about. I have been equally pleased to be the midwife, helping give birth to the words that capture the insights and experiences of God's work through David.

The authors are grateful to the following persons who read the manuscript and made helpful suggestions: Randall and Sara Brown, Willard and Doris Ferguson, Becky Ankeny, George and Dorothy Thomas, and Paul and Leona Thornburg. Each of these persons has been part of Friends mission work in Burundi in the past.

"Forgiveness means abandoning your right to pay back the perpetrator in his own coin, but it is a loss that liberates the victim. . . . Does the victim depend on the culprit's contrition and confession as the precondition for being able to forgive? There is no question that, of course, such a confession is a very great help to the one who wants to forgive, but it is not absolutely indispensable. Jesus did not wait until those who were nailing him to the cross had asked for forgiveness. He was ready, as they drove in the nails, to pray to his Father to forgive them and he even provided an excuse for what they were doing. If the victim could forgive only when the culprit confessed, then the victim would be locked into the culprit's whim, locked into victimhood, whatever her own attitude or intention. That would be palpably unjust."

        — Desmond Tutu

# 1

# THE POWER OF FORGIVENESS

**David, last week you said you would tell me about the terrible death of some of your students at the Kwibuka school. Could you tell me about it today?**

**Of course, Emmanuel. This is a difficult story for me to tell, but there are some important lessons to be learned from it.**

It was a beautiful morning in Burundi. I was with the students of Kwibuka Pastoral Training Center where I was the teacher. We were taking a break between classes, sitting in the sun on the steps of their dormitory. I was thinking about these bright students and those who had previously studied in the school.

The school was in its third year of operation, and we had already seen encouraging results among the two groups who had finished their year-long courses of study. The Friends churches in Burundi and Rwanda were growing rapidly, and there was a great need for trained leaders. Many of the church leaders had lost their lives in the violence that had plagued the countries, so the available leaders did not come close to meeting the need. The people of our churches were like sheep who were brought into the pen, but who had not been properly fed. We had taught the students how to discern God's leading in their lives and how to follow His direction. We also taught them to become prayer warriors, an essential tool in their new ministries. We stressed that the servants of the Lord must have a vision for ministry and must have the tools to accomplish it. We helped the students locate groups of people who had to walk for three hours or more each way to attend worship and to help these people plant churches. We then taught the students how to write a letter to local officials, requesting land for a church. We also taught them how to follow up on those who found the Lord, organize prayer and Bible study groups, and disciple these new believers.

It was a beautiful morning indeed. Yes, we had heard gunfire from Gitega earlier in the morning, but that was a common occurrence in Burundi. Gitega, a major provincial town, was only two miles away, so we usually were aware when there was trouble in the area. It was October 25, 1993, and Burundi's president, Melchior Ndadaye, had been assassinated four days before. Apparently, soldiers in the Burundi army, made up primarily of Tutsis, had done the killing. According to the twisted logic of Burundi politics, the two major ethnic groups in Burundi, Tutsi and Hutu, have felt they must do everything possible to keep the other group from gaining further power and influence. Ndadaye was Hutu, reason enough for Tutsis with power to put an end to his presidency before his term even began.

The struggles between the nation's ethnic factions seemed distant from us that day. Our task was to learn from God's Word how to be effective in the work of the church. Students had no desire to get involved in the battles among the ethnic and political groups. There were both Hutus and Tutsis enrolled in the school and as far as the students and I were concerned, that was the way it should be. We believed there was no difference in God's eyes between the two groups. We wanted our students to reach out to all Burundians with the Gospel, not limit their evangelism to one group.

Our pleasant conversation came to a sudden stop that morning. We heard someone coming up the roadway into the Kwibuka compound. There were no walls and gates to keep strangers out of what had been the headquarters for missionary work in previous decades. We had nothing to hide and knew of no reason to be afraid of the approaching group.

Within seconds it was obvious that the visitors had not come for a social visit, nor had they come for a tour of the school. There were about twenty in the group, some of them armed soldiers and some of them civilians. Although we couldn't tell their ethnic group as they approached, we later learned they were all Tutsis and they were on a mission to kill Hutus. We did not fear they had come for revenge, for in no way had the students and I been involved in any of the ethnic clashes.

We wouldn't have been surprised if the group had questioned us and harassed us, even accusing us of harboring persons whom they blamed for the violence against the Tutsis. But they asked no questions and made no accusations. They apparently thought we were all Hutus, but they were wrong about that. Three of the students were Tutsis.

From the time we realized the soldiers were heading toward the school and the time they began shooting, it couldn't have been more than a few seconds. There was no time to reason with the soldiers, no time to negotiate. We did what I suppose anyone would have done upon hearing the terrifying sound of automatic weapons. We scattered in every direction. I was sure some of the students would be killed and that I might be killed as well, but I knew I could do nothing to stop the assassins.

I ran from the scene of the butchering, wondering if the next bullet would be for me. In a bizarre way, it was like a childhood game of hide and seek, with one big difference: getting caught could mean the end of my life. I was so nearly overcome by fear and shock, it was all my legs could do to carry me across the open space to the building where I thought I could hide, a building that had been used to train young people in auto mechanics. The mechanics school had been closed when the missionaries had to leave in the 1980s and had remained locked, with many of the tools and auto parts still in place.

I unlocked and entered the shop door, hoping that the soldiers would assume the building was abandoned and pass on by. Just in case the soldiers might break into the building, I had to find a hiding place inside. I climbed into the pit where the mechanics could stand under a vehicle to drain the oil and do other work. An old vehicle was on top of the pit, so I hoped the soldiers might not see the pit and spot me under the car.

The gunfire continued while the soldiers moved through the compound looking for more victims. I had heard the guns many times before, but always from a distance. That day they were unbelievably loud. My efforts to hide seemed so useless, considering the power of the soldiers' weapons. At first I couldn't tell where the soldiers were and whether they would come and look in the shop building. As I huddled in the mechanics' pit, I could barely put a prayer together. "God protect me," was all I could manage.

It seemed at first that the soldiers might go on past the abandoned shop, but then I heard them coming toward the shop building. I could hear them speaking, trying to decide whether to come inside. As awful as the sounds of the guns had been, an even more terrifying sound was the shattering of the door as the soldiers knocked it down to gain entrance. I imagined Daniel hearing the sound of the grinding of the lion's teeth as he tumbled into the dungeon. But in minutes I experienced a Daniel-like deliverance. The soldiers only briefly looked inside and decided no one was there.

The footsteps echoed off into the distance. Soon there was no more gunfire. But I knew the soldiers could return at any time. So I stayed in the pit for an hour, for two hours, for three hours. What if the armed men were waiting in ambush for someone to emerge from hiding? I knew that could be the case, but I desperately wanted to go check on my students. Some might have escaped like I did. There was no way to know, and the risks of coming out of my hiding place seemed to be too great to ignore. So I stayed there for the rest of the day and the night. I was exhausted emotionally and physically, but there was no way to sleep without knowing the fate of the students and others at the compound.

By morning I could no longer bear to stay in the smelly shop. What had happened to my students and what about my family?

Had the soldiers gone looking in the homes in the area for Hutus? Would they know Felicity was Tutsi, and would they even care? Would they make her suffer for my escape? Finally, I was so desperately hungry I could no longer stay hidden in the shop.

I grabbed an old pair of mechanic's overalls in the shop, hoping I might not be recognized as I left the compound. It seemed futile to disguise myself, but I had to try. I imagined the soldiers spotting me, laughing at my silly disguise.

Where to go? Was there any place where I would be safe? Were the soldiers really after me, rather than the students? These and other thoughts raced through my mind. I made a quick decision not to go to the school building where the murders began, but to seek another hiding place. Where does one go when one's world has collapsed and one may be minutes away from death? Where does one go when the sound of machine guns can still be heard in the distance? Where does one go when one has no idea what has happened to his wife and three-month-old son?

I chose to go to my parents' home, thinking they might be able to protect me from the murderers or at least might know something about the fate of my wife and children. After all, my parents had survived more than one round of killings in the past. Adrenaline surged through my body as I raced the three miles to their house. When I entered their home, I could see equal parts of relief, joy, and alarm on my father's face. He said almost nothing and quickly directed me to the attic as the only possible hiding place in the house.

I settled into the dust and spider webs, relieved I had found part of my family alive and that I had another hiding place. Then it hit me. What if the soldiers came to the house? Of course they would look in the attic. Who was I kidding? They would definitely kill my parents for trying to hide me. Why had I put them in such danger? They had survived the killings in 1972, only to be put at risk by my attempt to hide.

Horrible memories flooded into my mind as I sat in the attic, memories of the deaths of our family members and friends twenty years before, when I was a young boy. The soldiers had been ruthless with their arrests. It seemed random at first, but then it became clear they were looking for educated Hutus, whom they considered to be a threat. My older brother was taken, as were many of my father's friends. Desperate to find out their fate, my father had ridden his bicycle into town, hoping he would be picked up and taken to where his loved ones were being held. He returned that afternoon with a very sad expression. He was not arrested, but he had no success in finding out anything about the fate of our loved ones. We were sure from his expression that we would not see these persons again. All he could manage to do that day was to sing a song of hope in the midst of dreadful evil: "I do not know what tomorrow holds for me, I live by faith." We later learned that the headmaster of our primary school, Binyoni, was among those arrested. Before he was shot, he too sang a song of assurance that he would soon be with Jesus. The song was "Jesus, I Come."

My agony over the possibility of endangering my parents by hiding in their house was interrupted by the sound of hushed, familiar voices below me. Praise the Lord! It was Felicity and our son, James, and they were fine. I came down to join them and we hugged each other and wept as we thanked the Lord for His protection and as we shared the information about the killings of the students and others in the neighborhood. There was some good news and lots of horrible news. My family members were spared, but so many others I knew and loved were dead. Although at the time we couldn't determine the ethnic group of the attackers, Felicity told me that the word was that they were Tutsis and they had come to find Hutus to kill, not knowing that some of the students were Tutsi.

The days dragged on, with no way of knowing whether we were still in danger. As a Tutsi, my wife felt she would be safe in our house. But I remained in my parents' attic, feeling fairly sure some of the bullets at the school had been meant for me, a well-known Hutu. Many in the area went to hide in the bush in the evening, fearing that other assassins might come at night. My father refused to hide, recalling his own agony over the loss of loved ones while his life was spared. He also feared someone might come looking for me and would burn the house, making it impossible for me to escape. He couldn't bear the thought of losing another son and was willing to do anything he could to protect Felicity and his grandson as well. My mother stayed in the house at night as well, since her rheumatism made the cold and the dew outdoors unbearable.

The days had turned into a week when I heard a voice say very clearly, "David, if you were meant to die, you would have been killed on the day when the students were massacred. No bullets came your way. What are you doing here?" There was no chance to decide if I was imagining the voice or hallucinating from the terrible experiences of the week. The voice was followed by what seemed like a video replay of an experience of the prophet Elijah.

Elijah was also in danger, as recorded in I Kings 19. The false prophets of Baal had been unable to call down fire to consume the sacrifices on the altar. God answered Elijah's prayer and the sacrifices and the entire altar were consumed. After Elijah ordered all the false prophets to be killed, Queen Jezebel promised that he would suffer the same fate as the dead prophets. Elijah fled to the desert, became deeply depressed and prayed that he might die. After angels came to encourage him, God Himself appeared and asked the question, "What are you doing here, Elijah?"

It was with relief and dread that I realized God was telling me to come out of my hiding place. After telling my parents about the voice and the vision, I said, "I must go back to Kwibuka and find out what has happened there. I can't bear the thought of not knowing for sure how many have been killed."

"Don't go," my father said. "Who knows who may still be lying in wait to attack anyone who comes to check. You've been spared so far. You can't do anything about those who have died."

"I must go, my father," I replied. "I'm sure that was what the Lord was telling me. We must begin to put our lives back together. We must trust God, who has delivered us so far."

I found a friend to go with me back to the school and our home. As we approached the buildings, things were frighteningly quiet. The strongest sensation we had as we arrived was the horrible smell of decomposing bodies. No one had dared to come bury the bodies. We entered our home, wondering if someone might be there to ambush us. But no one was there, and there were no bodies. Many of our belongings had been taken. Even the curtains from our windows were gone.

The next few days are a blur in my memory. We returned to the village and hired men to help bury the bodies. Wild dogs and hungry flies fought with each other to consume the bodies before we could get them buried. We buried the bodies we found, but soon realized from the smell that there were other bodies in the area. So we called for help to finish the job. In all, we found and buried 25 bodies. Some of the victims had lived some distance from the mission station. Apparently they had been wounded as they fled from Gitega and had made it only as far as Kwibuka before they died.

When the burials were finished and when it seemed clear there would be no other attacks, I began to suffer in a new way. In retrospect I can understand it was like the depression experienced by Elijah after he had escaped from Jezebel's wrath and had time to ponder his circumstances. I sat down and cried and cried. All I could think of were a whole series of "why" questions. Why did so many have to die, especially the students who had so much potential in God's work? Why had there been no warning that something like this might happen? Why hadn't God told us to flee? What had we done to make the informants bring the soldiers to our school? Why had the attackers gotten mixed up, killing two Tutsi students and sparing the life of a Hutu? Why, God, why?

My emotions swirled around in my body, going from grief, to horror, to anger, to fear, and to frustration. In despair, I wanted to renounce my calling to serve in the ministry. If God is in control of everything, was He not to blame for allowing this terrible thing to happen? Like Elijah I was nearly ready to ask God to take my life.

God told Elijah to go back the way he had come, and that's essentially the message God gave to me to lift me from the anger and depression that was beginning to consume me. I was being directed to come to terms with the killing episode, to seek out the ones who had been responsible for bringing the soldiers to Kwibuka. What an outrageous idea! Was I to talk with those who had been responsible for the death of these innocent ones? How could anyone do such a thing? Oh, yes. I knew the Sermon on the Mount. I had graduated from a Bible college. I had preached from these teachings of Jesus many times. I knew Jesus had told His followers to love their ene- mies, to do good to those who hated them, to bless those who cursed them, to pray for those who mistreated them. But did these teachings really apply to such blatant evil as this? Did Jesus not care about the suffering of these innocent ones? If I loved and forgave the killers, how would the grieving relatives of the dead ones feel? Did Jesus really intend for us to obey this teach- ing literally?

While I pondered these "hard teachings" of Jesus, I received forms from the local authorities, asking for the names of the dead and for information on who might be responsible. Of course I knew the students' names, and I also had recognized one of the local Tutsis who had brought the soldiers to Kwibuka. But I decided not to fill out the forms. I had no confidence that the authorities would apprehend those who had carried out the vio- lence. I felt sure that the persons involved in the killings would find out we had reported them and would come back to kill us to prevent us from testifying against them.

Then a new and amazing word came to me from the Lord. It was one thing to decline bringing charges against the killers. That was mostly done for self-protection. God told me to go the next step and actually forgive these enemies, as Jesus had taught. Forgive them? Yes. Was I to go to these persons and tell them I forgave them? Yes. Would that be easy? Of course not. Was God asking me to do this? Yes, He was.

While I was still arguing with myself about whether I could forgive the killers, I was in town and encountered Filbert, one of the two local persons who had led the group to Kwibuka. Before I could talk myself out of speaking to this man, I found myself greeting him and reaching out and shaking his hand. To my great surprise, these words came from my mouth, "By God's power, I forgive you for your part in bringing the soldiers to kill our students at Kwibuka."

Filbert looked as if I had struck him between the eyes. "What are you saying? You're badly mistaken. I was not involved at all in that incident." If Jesus' beloved follower Peter could not even admit that he was one of the disciples, how could I expect Filbert to admit he was the informer with the blood of my students on his hands?

"I'm not here to argue with you, Filbert," I responded. "I'm telling you I know you were one of those in the group. But I'm not accusing you either. I'm forgiving you. Jesus has asked me to forgive those who have wronged me, and by His power I'm doing exactly that."

My words had a dramatic effect on both of us. Filbert was completely overwhelmed and speechless, even though he couldn't bring himself to confess. I, in turn, was overwhelmed with joy and relief. I felt that a heavy load had been lifted from my back. I felt released. Peace spread through my body and spirit. Fear and anger gave way to boldness and love. It was like Saul in Damascus, when Ananias had prayed for him. Scales fell from Saul's eyes. He arose, was baptized, took food, and regained his strength. Scales fell from my eyes as well. I had only been able to see the evil in others, but my new eyes permitted me to see a person whom God loved and was willing to forgive. How could I not forgive someone who was freely being offered God's grace and forgiveness?

That simple handshake and those few words of forgiveness became a turning point in my life, pulling me away from the spirit of revenge which has overwhelmed the people of Burundi, and turning me toward the spirit of forgiveness. With renewed boldness, I was able to go to our churches and mission stations to see how people were getting along and to encourage them. I even went to Bujumbura to speak on the radio, giving words of encouragement and hope. My visits and words helped those in hiding to have the courage to return to their homes. From that point forward, the emphasis in my ministry expanded to include initiatives toward reconciliation and peace.

Later I heard about a similar experience of transformation experienced by a member of the "other" ethnic group, the Tutsis. This man, Nsabimana Johnson, was overwhelmed by hatred toward the Hutus, who had been responsible for killing his parents and other relatives, also in 1993. "I was full of hatred against every Hutu person," he later said. "I didn't want to talk again with a Hutu or be reconciled with them."

Johnson remained active in his church, still carrying with him the burden of hatred toward Hutus. Then he attended a retreat in the United States, sponsored by an organization committed to reconciliation. At the retreat he met Hutu Christians and with the help of skilled facilitators was able to study the Bible with the Hutus, to pray with them, and to discover they were people who genuinely loved God and were able to forgive others. Said Johnson, "By the Word of God and by the Holy Spirit, I was touched in my heart. I knew that if I didn't forgive those who had killed my family, I would never be free and happy in my life." He sought forgiveness for his hatred of Hutus. "Now, I am free," he reports, "and I love everybody without discrimination." (Stan Guthrie, *"Peacemaking," Discernment: A Newsletter of the Center for Applied Christian Ethics*, Wheaton College, Summer 2000, p. 1)

Nsabimana Johnson, a Tutsi, experienced the power of God that allowed him to replace hatred with forgiveness. I, a Hutu, experienced that same power of God to forgive the Tutsis who took the lives of those I loved. In both cases God had performed a great miracle of healing.

**David, do you sometimes have nightmares about that terrible night at Kwibuka, hiding in the mechanics' shop?**

**Yes, Emmanuel, sometimes the horror and fear of that experience comes back into my memories and my dreams. I hope you never have to go through anything like it. But God has given me wonderful healing from this tragedy.**

"Vengeance is a passion to get even. It is a hot desire to give back as much pain as someone gave you. . . . The problem with revenge is that it never gets what it wants; it never evens the score. Fairness never comes. The chain reaction set off by every act of vengeance always takes its unhindered course. It ties both the injured and the injurer to an escalator of pain. Both are stuck on the escalator as long as parity is demanded, and the escalator never stops, never lets anyone off."

—Lewis Smedes

# 2

# THE ROOTS OF DISTRUST IN THE DAYS OF THE KINGS

We humans tend to blame our troubles on others. Burundians are no exception. It serves our interests to blame the Europeans for bringing upon us all the evils of modern political and social history. From the sorry record of acquiring and exporting slaves to the carving up of the continent among the powerful European nations, a good case can be made for blaming colonization for the evils of the recent past.

In some parts of the continent, the story is almost that simple. Many of the African groups had lived in relative harmony within their territories and had found ways to trade and interact with other groups, with relatively minor episodes of violence. Then came the rape of the people and the land, with the capture and transport of large number of slaves. No one can think of the history of slavery in Africa, whether the early period under the Arabs, or the later European involvement, with anything but sadness and disgust.

The forced extraction of valued commodities is another part of the sad record of colonization. One of the more scandalous episodes involved the regime of King Leopold II of Belgium. In the Congo, traders coerced the indigenous people to collect the liquid from which rubber was made. It was well documented at the time that local people who were uncooperative or who did not gather their quota of rubber were tortured and mutilated, some of them by having their hands cut off.

As tempting as it might be to blame the Arabs and Europeans for the problems of Africa in the twentieth century, the roots of violent conflict in Burundi actually run too deep to be blamed entirely on the Germans, the Belgians, the French, or any of the other colonial powers. The phrase in Kirundi, *"Ganza Sabwa"* (the king [mwami] rules and reigns), suggests a tradition of remarkable stability and harmony. To some extent the long-standing monarchy in Burundi did hold the people together in harmony and unity. All people looked to the king and his royal symbols as their own. There was the royal drum, the karyenda. There were the royal tombs. There were the annual rituals (umu-ganuro), calling on their god (Imana) for a bountiful harvest. The phrase in Kirundi that best suggests the tradition of political sta-bility is *"Umwami aca amateka ntaca agasunikano"* (The king makes laws, he never makes troubles). (Rene Lemarchand, *Burundi: Ethnic Conflict and Genocide*, Woodrow Wilson Center Press, 1994, pp. 34-36)

The kings in Burundi based their legitimacy in part on the belief that they were born with a seed, a particular quality that made them superior to others and entitled them to continue the hereditary system of rule. In Europe this idea was called the "divine right of kings." This belief gave the kings of Burundi the freedom to rule and to extend their power to all areas of life, whether economically or socially. Kings, all of whom were Tutsis, ruled with the help of numerous chiefs and subchiefs. These local officials were responsible for the subdi-visions of the kingdom, which were known as chiefdoms and subchiefdoms. There were a few Hutu chiefs and slightly more Hutu subchiefs.

During the rule of the kings, people's wealth and power was most visible in the number of cattle owned and the amount of land they owned or controlled. Burundi's people gained their food and livelihood from tilling the land and from owning cattle, even though all the cattle as well as the land theoretically belonged to the king. In fact, the notion of idyllic harmony among the people and between the people and the king is not entirely accurate, for the king had the right to confiscate the cattle or the land from whomever he judged to be rebellious in one way or another. It was a serious punishment to have your riches confiscated by the king. In those days, some people believed it was better to be killed by the king, as sometimes happened, than to lose all your belongings. Hence, the old Kirundi saying, "It is better to be a grave than to be a dog," meaning that it is better to die than to be despised.

Because the cows in the early days of Burundi were one of the most visible evidences of wealth and because their ownership was more easily transferred than land, they had an important social function. At the time of a marriage, it was a cow that was normally given as a bride price. Cows were also a very important status symbol, in that everyone could see who had the largest number of cows and they knew these were the richest people. Having a lot of cows also meant having the greatest amount of land for their pasture and the largest number of workers to care for the cows. Thanks to the cows' manure, having lots of cows meant having fertile land and abundant crops. The person with cows was always respected and was referred to as *"Uwufise Ibihinda,"* a person with "things that make noise." Another interesting expression in Kirundi to describe a wealthy person is "a person whose belongings have made him deaf." This means that the moos of the cattle, the noise of the caretakers, and the comings and the goings of visitors make the rich person unable to hear the cry of the poor for help.

Just as the king had the right to confiscate cattle, he also had the right to reallocate the land to those who came to serve in his court. It was the custom for people to go to the king's court for weeks at time, doing work ranging from cooking and taking care of the cattle to cultivating the land and hunting. Some of these courtiers also provided entertainment for the royal household and assisted with the handling of disputes.

Most of what we know about the period of the kings before the Belgians arrived comes from oral histories. Oral histories can be both accurate and inaccurate. They are carefully transmitted from one generation to the next, but it is easy to pick and choose from these stories to develop a preferred version of reality. Those who wanted to blame the Germans and Belgians for modern interethnic conflict tended to overlook the indigenous sources of conflicts.

In the 1850s, following the death of Ntare Rugamba, the Burundian mwami at the time, there followed a period of internal discord and power struggles, none of which can be blamed on the Europeans. Most often the conflict originated among the members of the royal family and their supporters and opponents. The king would appoint princes to be his representatives in a variety of locations in the kingdom, permitting the extension of royal control over a greater territory. The system worked fine as long as the king's brothers and sons who governed under his authority were fully loyal to the crown, but this was not always the case.

Early political conflicts in Burundi bring to mind one of the characteristics of the cows in Burundi, which are the types with very large and heavy horns. It was not easy for these cows to enter into the *rugo*, the pen in which they were kept, since the gate leading to the enclosure was usually quite narrow. The cow had to turn its neck sideways, just like the maneuver you would perform if you wanted to get a big table through a door. Once inside the enclosure, the cows invariably got their horns tangled. Because of this experience with the cattle locking their horns, there is a saying, *"Ntazibana zidaku-bitana amahembe,"* meaning, "The cows that live together will lock their horns." The cattle did not fight, because the place was usually too small for that. What the owner would hear before the cows lay down to sleep would be the sound of the locking and unlocking of their horns. It is this Kirundi saying and the history of conflict on which it is based that provides the title for this book.

As long as they were subordinate to the king and ruled on his behalf in their territory, the "cows" got along fine. But cows and people are inclined to test each other's power and toughness. This is exactly what happened in the 1850s. Ntare Rugamba's sons had been ruling over various parts of an expanded Burundian kingdom. When Ntare died in about 1852, one of his sons, Mwezi Gisabo, inherited the throne. To consolidate his control over the kingdom, he attempted to replace his brothers, who had been governing various parts of the kingdom under their father's authority, with his sons, who might be expected to be more loyal than his brothers. The five decades of Mwezi's rule, before and during the German "ownership" of Burundi, were characterized by constant battles within the royal family. Mwezi and his sons fought with his brothers and nephews, who had been appointed as governors by his father and were not willing to surrender their power.

The simplistic version of Burundi's history is that every conflict can be explained on the basis of distrust between the Tutsi and Hutu. But the conflict within the royal family during Mwezi's rule was over territory and power, not over ethnic differences. The princes were all Tutsi, but many of those who served in the royal governmental system were Hutus and some of the chiefs and subchiefs were also Hutus. Alliances were formed and lines drawn over issues of power and control, not over the relatively minor distinctions between Hutu and Tutsi. (Lemarchand, pp. 37-39)

**Emmanuel, let me tell you a story from the early days in Burundi. We like to think it was a time of peace and goodwill, but it was also a time of greed and selfishness. Let me tell you about a clever person who gained favor with the king.**

There was once a man who was very poor. Even though he was wise and hospitable, he was so despised and so miserable that his only chance of personal improvement was to go serve in the king's court. By serving there for several weeks or months, he could expect to be given a cow, for this was the custom. Although everyone who went to the king's court in those days was expected to carry the best gift from his/her labor, the poor man had nothing of value to give to the king's officials. But he went to the court in spite of having no gift, hoping he would be rewarded in some way. It took him many days before other people at the court noticed his talents and mentioned these to the king. The poor man was relieved when the king finally asked him to entertain him with his clever stories. These tales were about a mythical figure called Samandari who lived at the king's court and who also was clever and had answers to every question. The king liked the stories about Samandari and continued calling the poor man to entertain him.

Soon the poor man became known as the most talented entertainer in the king's court. In due time, as was his custom, the king offered the poor man a cow, but the poor man refused, much to the surprise of everyone in the court. Instead, the poor man asked the king to call him in when he sat with his chiefs and elders to make decisions about important cases in the kingdom. The king was as surprised as everyone else at the poor man's request and readily agreed to call the man in for the next important case. Soon a major land dispute arose between two neighbors. The case was far too difficult to be settled by the local elders, so it was brought to the king.

When the king and all his elders took their seats at the public place, the king remembered the request of the poor man and called on him to join the officials in considering the case. The man came and leaned close to the ear of the king as if he were giving advice to the king. This surprised the chiefs and elders and made them wonder why the king would ask advice from this poor man. They were especially surprised that the king knew the man by name. From that time forward, all the people respected and feared the poor man because they believed he had special influence with the king. After all, they had seen the poor man speak directly into the king's ear. As a result, the chiefs brought many gifts to the poor man, to win his favor. They gave him cows and land, so that he would be kind to them and give good reports to the king on their behalf. The poor man became very rich and powerful.

**Emmanuel, what can you learn from this story?**

**It sounds like the lesson is that the clever person always finds a way to prosper.**

**That may be true, to a point, but there's more than that to learn from the story. Our ancestors were thought to live in a time of peaceful cooperation. They never fought one another, so it seems. But there was much at the time to divide people. They always wanted more cattle and land. Their power was in what they possessed and the connections they had to those more powerful. Can we Burundians not find a way to value more than our posessions and power?**

"And so we went to our inn again, and there were two desperate fellows fighting so that none durst come nigh to part them, but I was moved in the Lord's power to go to them, and when I had loosed their hands, I held one of them by one hand and the other by the other hand; and I showed them the evil of their doings, and convinced them, and reconciled them to each other that they were loving and very thankful, so that people admired at it."

—George Fox

# 3

# THE ROOTS OF UNITY AND HEALING IN THE DAYS OF THE KINGS

The recent decades of severe violence in Burundi have given birth to many myths and misconceptions. One of these is the false notion that the major ethnic groups in Burundi—Hutu, Tutsi, and Twa—are and always have been distinct ethnic groups with irreconcilable differences. Those who know little about Burundi's history and culture attribute recent conflicts to "tribalism." Europeans and Americans like to think that tribal differences and tensions account for all the discord that came forth during the colonial era and since independence. According to this myth, the ethnic groups of Africa carried their cultural distinctives into the modern era and have continued to be unable to get along with one another. Of course, Europeans and Americans have not been any more effective in dealing with their cultural differences without resorting to violence. The history of Europe and North America is punctuated with one bloody war after another.

Indeed, tribalism is not a sufficient explanation for Burundi's experiences of the last century. The idea that there are irreconcilable differences among Burundi's ethnic groups is one of the major obstacles to reconciliation and it is important to put to rest some of the misinformation:

## LANGUAGE

Language is one of the most important indicators of cultural unity or disunity. Look at most countries in Africa and you will find dozens of different languages and dialects and these tend to divide the people. Not in Burundi. All Burundians speak Kirundi. In fact, most can understand Kinyarwanda, the language of our ethnic "cousins" in Rwanda. Moreover, most of us speak Swahili, which further ties us together and to the neighboring people around us. And in modern times, many of us have learned the European languages, especially French and English, further breaking down internal and external walls. In short, we are one people, who speak several languages.

## PHYSICAL APPEARANCE

One of the unfortunate misunderstandings of the people of Burundi is the stereotyping of ethnic groups by appearance, much of this coming from the colonizers, who felt they needed some way of distinguishing one group from the other. The most common stereotype is that all Tutsi are tall and all Hutu are short. Other physical stereotypes are: small nose, large nose; slim, bulky; slender cheeks, big cheeks; light skin, darker skin. Another stereotype is one of vocation: Tutsi are thought to have been herders of cattle, the Hutu to be cultivators. Burundians know that our history is much more complex than that. There are so many exceptions to the stereotypes that they serve no function. You simply cannot look at someone in Burundi and know what ethnic group they are from. Can an outsider arrive in Northern Ireland and tell by appearance who belongs to which side of the "Catholic" and the "Protestant" divide? Of course not. Nor can an outsider accurately tell who is a Hutu and Tutsi. We are fundamentally one people.

## HISTORY

Burundians cannot blame all the ethnic misperceptions on the outsiders. The fact is that the killings of the past generation cry out for excuses and explanations and many of these can be found in our culture. There were tensions between people, there were outbreaks of violence, there was exploitation, but most of this was not primarily ethnic. Our history cannot be explained through the framework of an alien minority invading and exploiting a native majority. We probably originated from a number of other parts of Africa, came here to Burundi and developed as one people, with many differences.

## GEOGRAPHY AND OCCUPATIONS

If language, culture, and history do not inevitably divide us, neither do geography and occupations. In some parts of Africa, there are rivers, mountains, deserts, forests, and lakes that separate people into distinct and sometimes hostile groups. This is not the case in Burundi. Ours is a small, mountainous country of some 28,000 square kilometers, about the size of Maryland in the United States. Lake Tanganyika forms most of our western border. It connects us with our neighbors, but doesn't divide us internally. The climate along the lake is more tropical than in the mountains, but we still do not have the extreme differences of climate and geography of many of our neighboring countries. Although some of the mountainous areas cannot be farmed, most of the country will grow crops and people are scattered uniformly throughout the country. Livestock can be raised in almost all areas. There are no drastic divisions among the sectors of the country.

## POLITICAL STRUCTURE

An even greater source of unity in Burundi's history is in the political structure. There are many forms of governance in traditional African cultures. Most often there were chiefs over relatively small areas, with no level of authority above the chiefs to mediate disputes and differences. Burundi was one of a relatively small number of monarchies in Africa. Similar to the monarchies in Europe at the time, the king possessed total power over the subjects and the local officials, who ruled at his pleasure. The Kirundi phrase that described the king's authority was *"Kuvukana imbuto"* (he was born with a seed in his hand). The king was seen as a kindly father figure, from whom one might hope to receive some personal favor as well as protection and stability in the land.

Under the king's ultimate authority, there was a group of princes with considerable power, called the Ganwa. While they sometimes struggled with the king on the one hand and the chiefs below them in power, they were not identified with either the Hutu or Tutsi. Below the Ganwas in power were the chiefs and subchiefs, with authority over various provinces, communes, and zones. Also operating under the king's authority, there was another level of social and political leadership, distinct from the system of chiefs and subchiefs. It was not a structure of administration, nor a group of elite people, but a system concerned mainly with the safeguarding of peace and conflict management. It was known as the cadre of elders, *"Abashingantahe."* The elders were both men and women and were ethnically diverse. Whenever there were problems in the villages related to land disputes, theft, or violence, these elders were called on to administer judgments and give advice. The most common disputes involved land, since land was so crucial for the livelihood and status of the people. This is why, in our culture, whenever conflicts arise between two people, the first inquiry is whether or not those people share the same land boundary, *"Hari akarimbi musangiye?"*

## PEACEMAKING TRADITION

Among the elders were a few who had the particular function of peacemaker. These were known as *"Gahuzamiryango"* (the reconcilers of families). These elders were required to be people with a good reputation in the community, those who would not accept bribes, those who never look at the Burundi community in terms of ethnic affiliation. They were described as mediators and those who were able to satisfy everyone equally, *"Buzuriza bose."* The king himself sought and received their help and wisdom in his court cases. Thanks to their wisdom, on numerous occasions they averted potential frontier wars between chiefdoms, quarrels between rival royal family members, and major disputes among families. During precolonial times, there were no great battles attributable to the ethnic divisions, and it was probably because of the role of the designated peacemakers in Burundi society.

The peacemaking elders handled the many conflicts that were brought to their attention and saw that everyone was treated justly. Their philosophy was *"Ukuri kuvugirwa ahagaragara"* (The truth is proclaimed in public) and *"Utara mu nda ugatarura ibiboze"* (You keep things in the stomach and they make you sick). They met with disputants in a public place, asking the accuser and the accused to sit in front of them and tell his or her stories, starting with the accuser. They then asked for clarifications, seeking the truth from the contradicting facts as shared by the opponents. They then retreated privately to seek a consensus about the veracity of the statements brought forward. In pronouncing the final verdict, they used a small stick, about two feet long, which they occasionally hit on the ground as they told the two people when one's "truth" had fallen short of the other one's "truth." They always sought and worked for harmony between the disputants themselves and among the community as a whole.

Among the more challenging cases brought to the peacemaking elders were those dealing with the traditional system of donating a cow, *"Ubugabire,"* and leasing a piece of land *"Ubugererwa"* to a needy person, in return for servanthood. This system, with its great potential for exploitation, persisted until quite recently and was the focal point of many conflicts in the past.

The peacemaking role of elders is one of the most important legacies of Burundi's culture. This and other parts of our culture simply do not support the idea of a permanently divided people, unable to live in peace for centuries in the past. We are a people of peace, who, unfortunately, have descended into being a people of war. Such is the tragedy of my beautiful land.

**David, I've never really heard much about our tradition of peacemaking. Can you explain more about how it worked?**

**Emmanuel, let me tell you about two families who were able to find healing in the midst of their hatred and distrust. You will hear that some conflicts simply cannot be solved. That may be true. But this story shows us that many long-standing disputes can be solved successfully and our people have a strong tradition of doing this.**

Once upon a time, Mukamakare ("One who milks early morning") gave birth to a baby boy and she named him Bazompora ("They will avenge me"). The boy grew up without a father and was saddened by the unexplained hatred that was so apparent between his family members and their neighbor's family. He wondered whether his father might have been killed by a buffalo, since in those days there were a lot of game parks in which the villagers organized themselves and hunted with their dogs.

Bazompora's neighbors had a boy of the same age as Bazompora. His name was Ndabahagamye ("I am in their throats"). The two boys used to play together when their mothers had gone to gather firewood in the forest. The two boys became very good friends, but didn't understand the warnings of their mothers that they should not eat roasted sweet potatoes from each other's houses.

One day, Ndabahagamye's father disappeared. The only explanation for the man's disappearance was that a relative of Bazompora had killed him while he was chasing a gazelle. This speculation about the reason for the death made the relationship between the two families even worse than it had been before. The hatred and suspicion was so evident that everyone in the neighborhood knew about it.

After the two boys grew up, they came to understand why their families had become enemies. Bazompora learned that during the time when he was still in his mother's womb, a terrible thing happened. His father and the other men of the village went to steal cattle from a village where Ndabahagamye's cousins lived, but Bazompora's father never returned. Bazompora's mother was pregnant, so she did not get to fully grieve for her husband. She hoped that her unborn child would be a strong man and take revenge for her husband. Even though there was no evidence her husband had been killed by a member of Ndabahagamye's family, there was strong suspicion and distrust between the two families. Both families' suspicions were fueled by the many stories each side told about acts of hatred and violence from the other family members. Bazompora and Ndabahagamye were constantly reminded that they must never let down their guard around the members of their neighboring family.

Things seemed hopeless between the two families. The two young men who once had been the closest of friends soon became bitter enemies. One evening as they were in a drinking place they quarreled over a pot of beer. A terrible fight broke out and they spilled the drink on everyone around them. Had it not been for the elders who came between them, the two young men might have killed each other. It was clear to the people around them that the reason for the fight was not really beer. It was something from deep within, which no one could comprehend. The wrestling was so intense, the blows so hard, that a large crowd gathered.

The bad relationship between Bazompora and Ndabahagamye went on for many years. But eventually they began to feel that they could no longer stand living in such a situation. One of the factors that contributed to this realization was seeing the destructive effects of this ill will among their children. How could the children be participants in and victims of something they didn't even understand? The two men became troubled and restless. In fact, Bazompora began to have stomach pains, which he thought were due to his frequent sleepless nights. He was constantly on edge, fearing that the relatives of Ndabahagamye might attack him and his family. Likewise, Ndabahagamye began to have a lot of headaches and attributed these to his sadness that his best childhood friend was now his worst enemy.

It was the custom in their village for certain men to slaughter cows after the harvest and to call on the villagers to pay for their share of the meat. It was a great time of celebration, as people met and talked while waiting for their portions of the meat. Children watched while some of the men showed their manliness by eating raw meat. The women watched carefully to be sure the men divided the meat equally. Even the cow's tongue was cut into dozens of equal pieces!

It was during one of these occasions when cows were being slaughtered that Bazompora and Ndabahagamye happened to be assigned to the same duty in preparing the carcasses of the cows. Their task was to clean out the intestines of the cows. At first they were reluctant to work together and wondered if someone was plotting to bring them together. After working silently together on the unpleasant task, they each began to see the similarity between the waste material they were cleaning from the cow and the anger and bitterness inside each of them toward the other. Without even needing to speak of the vivid lesson they were learning from the insides of the cows, they began to think of ways they could deal with the awfulness inside their own spirits. In fact, before the project was done, they had agreed to meet and to work on settling their hatred and enmity once and for all.

As they began to talk about the suspicions and fears that divided their families, they uncovered a lot of misinformation and assumptions that had circulated between their families. Even though at the time no one thought their differences were the result of being from the two different ethnic groups, Hutu and Tutsi, they began to realize some of their distrust came from suspicions between the people of these two groups.

While the meat was still being divided among the villagers, Bazompora and Ndabahagamye resolved that they would talk to the elders about their desire to solve their conflicts and make peace between their families. Some people had spotted the two men sitting together in the shade and talking. Everyone wondered what was going on between them, for their feud was well known to everyone in the village. It was obvious something unusual was happening, for the two "enemies" already had smiles on their faces as they began talking with the elders.

One elder was known as an especially effective peacemaker. Whenever he passed by people engaging in disagreement he would stop and try to reconcile them. If the matter were too complicated for him to handle, he would invite them to a meeting with his fellow elders to hear them and help settle their disputes. This in fact was the reason the whole community respected him and had accepted him into the eldership system. He was respected by everyone. This man took special interest in the case.

Before the elder left to go home with his bag full of meat, he urged the two men to continue working out the differences between their families. He told them not to allow themselves to be distracted by others in the family who might undermine this initiative and fan the flames of hatred. He pled with them to set aside the memories of traumatic events of violence committed by the other family. He promised to tell the other elders about their decision to reconcile themselves and get rid of all the schemes of revenge among their family members. He said he would ask the elders to prepare for a special day of reconciliation. This was to be a big event, a day of celebration for the whole community.

The tradition of peacemaking in the culture called for an elder to meet with each of the enemy families to impress on them that it was essential that they be reconciled. The elder would ask them to stop the cycle of violence and remove the walls dividing them by acknowledging that both sides had wronged the other. The elder would declare that the day had come to forgive one another and rebuild a peaceful relationship based on love, understanding, trust, and cooperation.

When the reconciliation day arrived, all the villagers came down the valley, from old to young, women with their babies on their backs or on their breasts, elders with their special sticks, taking their position in the village market place. When the people had all gathered, the chief elder gave a long speech about the peacemaking traditions of Burundians. The elder explained the custom of hitting his stick on the ground to pronounce the village's blessings on the confessions from the representatives of the previously hostile families.

With the explanations finished, the chief elder summoned Bazompora and Ndabahagamye to stand before him. In an atmosphere of solemnity, he invited them to rid themselves of the enmity between their families. He called on them to denounce the wrong they had perpetrated over the years and to agree to enter into a new relationship based on a mutual love and respect. He called on them to ceremonially wash themselves, symbolizing the cleansing from everything that had produced the hatred between the families. As the two men washed, they were thinking about ridding their bodies and spirits of the kinds of distasteful material they found inside the cows. The cleansing ceremony publicly solidified the determination of the two men to change their hearts and minds. The elder then called upon the people of the whole village to bear witness to a new and healthy relationship between the families and to do all they could to help make it a lasting peace. The Kirundi word used by the elder was "kunywana," meaning "to reconcile." The chief elder then brought the ceremony to a close by calling on the crowd to treat these families as friends, not enemies.

The ceremonial cleansing represented the removal of the hatred, murderous actions, wrong thinking, deceit, and selfish ambitions, which had poisoned the families' relationship. The bright sunshine symbolized a new way of looking at one another, thus fostering a reestablishment of a healthy relationship. When the peacemaking ceremony had finished, there arose a great shout of joy. The people raised their voices in acclamation, clapping their hands enthusiastically. The elders led the way up the hill to a place where a big container was prepared. The two families poured their pots of beer into the single huge pot, symbolizing the coming back together of the two families. Bazompora and Ndabahagamye, as the heads of the two families, took straws from a decorated bowl and drank from the pot together. Members of both families took their turns in the ceremonial drinking. When all the family members had sipped from the pot, the elders declared the two families reconciled and took a drink themselves. There followed a great celebration, with abundant amounts of food for everyone—yams, beans, greens, sweet potatoes, and several kinds of meat. Everyone was happy. Those who had musical instruments rushed home to bring them and played a rhythm to which everyone danced in jubilation.

**David, is this just a story, or did this kind of peacemaking really occur in our culture?**

**Oh yes, Emmanuel, this happened many times, in many families and between many enemies. But like some of our other traditions, as time went on, not everyone practiced these customs. It became easier to let the rivalries and hatreds continue on from one generation to another. The killings in our lifetimes are a sorry witness to the failure to practice our people's rich tradition of peacemaking.**

"He who cannot forgive another breaks the bridge over which he must pass himself."

—George Herbert

# 4

# THE ROOTS OF DISTRUST AND HEALING IN THE COLONIAL PERIOD

It's quite an amazing thing for Africans to read about the discovery and exploration of the interior of Africa. I suppose it must be something like Native Americans, whose ancestry goes back many centuries, to hear about the "discovery" of North America by Europeans. My ancestors in Central Africa weren't in need of being discovered and gained little from the arrival of the Europeans. David Livingstone, the most famous of the European explorers of Africa, was interested in the penetration of the continent with the Gospel of Christ, but many of the other explorers and the traders that followed him were motivated almost entirely by wealth and power, not by love and evangelism.

The coastline of Africa had been staked out by the European nations for a very long time, this "occupation" symbolized by coastal forts from which slaves were exported. But what we now call Burundi was mercifully distant from most of the European slave activity. The Arab slave traders had moved far inland but the Europeans at first limited their contact with Africa to the coast and a few large rivers. Portugal, France, and England had been active in making these coastal claims and for many years there seemed to be plenty of land in this huge continent to satisfy the Europeans' greed.

The first significant European claims reaching deeply into the interior were those of King Leopold II of Belgium. His small country had not established claims along the coast, so Leopold began to look inland for possible land and wealth. Leopold took note of the explorers' reports of abundant resources in the Congo basin and in the 1870s formed a non-governmental association to open the "Dark Continent," as it was commonly called, to what the Europeans called "civilization." Leopold's stated goals were not all that bad. He said he wanted to put an end to the Arab slave trade in the interior, to make it possible for missionaries to penetrate the interior, and to open the area to trade. Leopold said, "The most intelligent of our youth demand wider horizons on which to expend their abounding energy, our working population will derive from the virgin regions of African new sources of energy and render more in exchange." (Eugen Weber, *A Modern History of Europe*, New York: W.W. Norton and Co., 1971, p. 739) Of course, Leopold was thinking primarily about the desires and needs of the Europeans. What about the effects of colonization on Burundi's intelligent and ambitious people?

King Leopold's claims in the Congo basin certainly did not yield instant wealth, but they did cause other Europeans to begin thinking about making similar claims in the continent's interior. Groups in France and Germany began to call on their governments to follow the lead of the Belgians. In northern Africa, France took control of Tunis and Britain took control of Egypt. Acquiring land was not the only goal. Europeans at the time believed their prosperity depended on the strength of their fleet and its success in carrying on trade. No European nation would permit rival powers to trade within the areas they claimed. So this mindset meant that every claim of a rival must be matched by similar claims for one's own nation. In this atmosphere of rivalry and competition, German Chancellor Otto von Bismarck convened the International Colonial Conference at Berlin, in late 1884.

To an African, it's astounding to think about the heads of state sitting around a table in Berlin, deciding which unclaimed parts of our continent would go to which nation. It brings to mind the image of high stakes gambling, with the futures of Africans going to the most clever players. Officially the conference in Berlin was supposed to place limits on European colonialism. It was agreed that freedom of navigation was to be assured in the Niger and Congo river basins. It was also agreed that European nations should not establish colonies without notifying the other European powers and without demonstrating effective occupation of the claimed area. None of the officials at the conference apparently thought much about whether the Africans in these territories were agreeable to the acquisitions.

One of the major outcomes of the Berlin conference was to recognize the claims of King Leopold in the Congo basin, an area to which Leopold had now given the misleading name, the Congo Free State. The "free" part was meant to refer to freedom of navigation of the river and freedom of trade in the area. Actually, Leopold had no intention of allowing free trade in the area, and he certainly had no desire to assure the continued freedom of activity for the indigenous people. As time went on, Leopold's plan for freedom became clearer. It was to be freedom for Belgian traders to gather all the natural resources they could and freedom for these traders and entrepreneurs to force the local people to cooperate.

Another result of the Berlin conference was to give the appearance of legitimacy to the newest European colonies in Africa. As the host of the conference, German Chancellor Bismarck was able to gain support for his establishment of the German colonies along the African perimeter—Togo and Cameroun in West Africa, South West Africa, and what came to be called German East Africa. The Sultan of Zanzibar had controlled the coastal part of this eastern area, later called Tanganyika and then Tanzania, but the Arabs were not present at the Berlin Conference, so their claims were ignored. Since

Leopold's claims stopped at a line between Lake Albert (now the western border of Uganda) and Lake Tanganyika (now Burundi's western border), Germany drew the boundaries of German East Africa all the way from the east coast to the eastern edge of the Congo Free State. The explorers had done some mapping of the interior, so with a few lines drawn on the maps, my ancestors became German subjects in 1885.

Of course, it was one thing to draw lines on a map and quite another to establish control over what the Germans began calling Urundi, or most often Ruanda-Urundi, combined with our twin country to the north. Until the Germans established a military station on Lake Tanganyika in 1896, calling it Usumbura, this was a German colony only on the maps. Arab slave traders still had a free hand in the area. And until the German Richard Kandt began a detailed survey of the territories, the Germans knew little about the geography of this part of German East Africa. My ancestors, of course, knew the area very well.

By some stretch of the imagination, one might say that the German acquisition of Burundi was a unifying force. If one subscribes to the myth that the indigenous people in Burundi were constantly at war among themselves, German occupation might be thought of as a peacemaking gesture. It is true that the arrival of the Germans was the beginning of the end of the activity of the Arab slave traders, but one might ask whether the Europeans could be expected to bring about greater peace and justice than the Arabs. Mwami Mwezi IV considered the Germans to be enemies, just as he had previously resisted the activities of the Arab slave traders. He saw little benefit from the arrival of the first missionaries, members of the White Fathers order of the Catholic Church, and did what he could to hinder their work, just as he tried to block the efforts of the German troops. But ultimately the spears and arrows of Mwezi's warriors were no match for the German firearms. Mwezi surrendered and signed the Treaty of Kiganda, permitting complete freedom of access to the Germans and the

Catholic missionaries. In exchange for recognition of their sovereignty, the Germans declared the Mwami to be the King of Burundi, a somewhat redundant gesture, since the Mwami was already King of Burundi.

Germany's stay in Burundi was short, for she had very little capacity to protect German East Africa during World War I. Belgian troops moved quickly and easily into Ruanda-Urundi and the League of Nations authorized Belgium to retain control over Burundi after the war as a League "mandate." The word *mandate* was a convenient diplomatic term for the spoils of war. Belgium has left a more lasting mark on Burundi than the Germans, for the Belgians were present in our land for nearly half a century, until the time of independence on July 1, 1962.

The seventy-five years of German and Belgian occupation did little to bring peace and unity to Burundi. Rather, the European legacy is one of conflict and disunity. The Germans and Belgians viewed their colony as a potential source of income, with no intention of investing in its development beyond the bare minimum to control it and to obtain exportable commodities. Local people were forced to perform unpaid labor for the Europeans. One might have called this a form of taxation, or considering what King Leopold had been doing in the Congo Free State, one might have thought of it as involuntary servitude. These practices of the Europeans disrupted the capacity of people to provide for their own needs and introduced conflict and disorder. The presence of the Europeans perpetuated the long-standing rivalry among local princes as these princes sought to win recognition and favors from the Europeans.

The Europeans did not set out to destroy and destabilize Burundi's culture, but some of the Western innovations had that result. For example, it was good to make schools available to Burundians, but the schools had the negative impact of undermining the traditional authority of the elders. Those who graduated from the schools were regarded as wise people, at least by the Belgians, whether or not they had the kind of wisdom that characterized the elders in our traditional system. Those who gained an education gained almost automatic recognition in the cadre of elders, even if they had cheated to get their grades in school or even if they had gained admission to the school in an inappropriate manner. The schools were essentially European in their curriculum, with little or no attention to local cultural values and no attempt to include the prevailing local language, Kirundi, or the regional language, Swahili. Use of the French language meant the use of books printed in Europe, which meant that nothing of African history and culture was taught in the schools.

The Belgians introduced coffee to Burundi in 1932. The crop was very well suited to the higher elevations in Burundi, as was apparent from the success of coffee production in the highlands of Kenya. Coffee continues to be a major source of earnings for Burundi, but from the beginning, the system of coffee production was not structured beneficially for the people of Burundi. Large Belgian companies developed and operated the coffee plantations and controlled the export and marketing process. People were forced to work on the plantations, with little if any compensation. Later the government required property owners to plant and care for coffee on their land, though they were allowed to keep the proceeds from selling the coffee.

The Europeans also introduced money to Burundi, overturning the traditional economic systems of exchange built around cows and land. Money had some benefits, but it disrupted existing systems of exchanges and existing social relationships and began to draw people away from reliance on the land.

Those Burundians who place their trust in Christ as their Savior and Lord have a great appreciation for one of the results of colonization, the coming of the missionaries. Since Belgium is a predominantly Catholic country, many of the missionaries were Catholic and to this day there are many more

Catholics than Protestants in Burundi. Some of the missionaries concentrated on evangelization, while others were involved with education, health care, and training in such work as carpentry, tailoring, and mechanics. Even though a number of different Protestant missions were established in Burundi, this has not been a source of division and discord. The mission groups were able to agree on different areas in which to work. The result of this mission work has been the large number of Burundians who identify themselves as Christians, which most definitely has been a unifying factor.

Probably the most difficult challenge for missionaries during the colonial period was trying to understand and deal with the rivalry between the ethnic groups. Some missionaries decided to ignore it as if it were not there; others considered it too sensitive to even discuss. By and large, it is probably accurate to say that the missionaries recognized ethnicity as a potential destabilizing factor in Burundi, but did not understand its complexities very well and did not know how to deal with it.

**David, I've heard a little about some of our traditional religions. Could you help me understand whether these long-standing beliefs contributed to unity or disunity in Burundi?**

**I'll try, Emmanuel, but I don't claim to be an expert on the subject.**

Burundians had a traditional religion called Kubandwa, in which the key figure was a man called Kiranga or Ryangombe, who was believed to be a mediator between God (Imana) and the people. Even the king who was respected as the "Father of Burundians" (Sebarundi), bowed before the Kiranga. Basically, everyone participated in the worship of the "God of Burundi" (Imana y'l Burundi) under the leadership of the Kiranga and his helpers, called Ibihweba. It was believed that the spirits of the ancestors were present whenever people gathered in those ceremonies, which usually took place at night.

Imana was considered to be an all-powerful being, able to give children to barren women, protect the vulnerable, and provide for the needy. People recognized their allegiance to God by the way they named their children. Some were given names like Hakizimana: God saves; Niyonzima: God is alive or God is the living one (which is my name); Nduwayo: I belong to Him. In addition to their belief in the goodness of God, Burundians believed in an evil being who did nothing but cause death. This powerful being, called Death (Urupfu), could come any time and indiscriminately kill young children as well as old people. In an attempt to avoid death, some parents gave names to their children like Ruribikiye: Death is keeping him; Rurihafi: Death is near her, etc. The idea was that Death could not take away what already belonged to him!

**That's interesting, David, but did Christianity come along and undermine these traditional beliefs that united our culture?**

**I wouldn't say so, Emmanuel. Christianity, more so than our traditional religion, teaches us to love one another, even to love our enemies. Christ transforms us to live in loving ways to those around us. Of course, Christians have not always done this, but that's not the fault of Christianity, just in the way we live it out.**

**Could I ask you a question on another subject, David? Do you think the Europeans deliberately brought division between the Hutus and Tutsis in Burundi, by giving special favors to the Tutsi, especially by giving them the most positions in the colonial government?**

Well, Emmanuel, that's a tough subject. I don't think the Europeans had anything to gain by stirring up conflict between the Hutus and Tutsis. The conflict was already there, though it was not as drastic as some outsiders have thought. There were all sorts of divisions among our people and it was seldom just a matter of Tutsi versus Hutu. But I think it's accurate to say that the Europeans used ethnicity as a simplistic way to select those to whom they gave leadership responsibility. In our traditional culture, leadership was based on wisdom and giftedness. The Europeans didn't try to identify the most gifted Tutsis and Hutus to reward with opportunities. By and large, they took the easy way out and decided to give the Tutsis preference in the schools and to give them the most rewarding positions in the government. The Europeans did not invent ethnicity, but they set in motion an imbalanced system of power and privilege. As long as the Belgians remained in power, they were able to keep the conflict somewhat in control. Sadly, it wasn't long after they left that ethnic conflict exploded.

David, you have written about the Berlin Conference. There is a song I've heard on Burundi Radio about our country being divided up. I think the person who wrote and recorded the song, Nkeshimana, is no longer living. One of the lines from the song is, "I'm taking Nyamirembe for myself." This seems to be talking about dividing up Burundi, but is it really about the greedy division of all of this part of Africa by the Europeans at the Berlin Conference?

That's very perceptive of you, Emmanuel. I think you could be right. The surface meaning of the song is about the division of Burundi's various areas among our chiefs and sub-chiefs. The composer may not have known much about the details of the carving up of Africa, but I think he may well have been talking about the greed of our own leaders and the Europeans at the same time. Greed is not European or Burundian, it's human, and really a reflection of human sinfulness.

A friend of mine gave me the words of the song in Kirundi:

Mu Kukigabura Wamenga Babaroze

Mboneko ngo "Ndatwaye Nyamirembe"

Majengo ngo "Ndatwaye Nyabitare"

Masabarakiza ngo "Ndatwaye uwa Makira"

Niyonzima ngo "Ndatwaye I wa Murore"

Shiramanga ngo "Ndatwaye Nyarunazi"

Urantunga mugenzi, urantunga.

Niyonzima was one of the greedy chiefs in the song. Do you claim him as your ancestor?

Oh no, Emmanuel, I don't think I have the blood of chiefs in my family line. As you know, mine is a fairly common name in Burundi.

And here are the words in English:

They Divided It As If They Were Bewitched

Mbonego said, "I'm taking Nyamirembe for myself"

Majengo said, "I'm taking Nyabitare for myself"

Masabarakiza said, "I'm taking the hill of Makira for myself"

Niyonzima said, "I'm taking the area of Murore for myself"

Shiramanga said, "I'm taking Nyarunazi for myself"
Be kind to me, my friend, be kind to me.


**The closing line of the song is interesting, Emmanuel. It's almost as if our culture, and certainly the culture of colonialism is tolerant of greed, as long as each of us has a chance to get our share of the take. The singer is saying, "Be kind to me," I want to get a piece of the pie as well.**

"Through the medium of prayer we go to our enemy, stand by his side, and plead for him to God. Jesus does not promise that when we bless our enemies and do good to them they will not despitefully use and persecute us. They certainly will. But not even that can hurt or overcome us, so long as we pray for them. . . . We are vicariously doing for them what they cannot do for themselves."

—Dietrich Bonhoeffer

# 5

# CHRISTIAN MISSIONS AS A SOURCE OF UNITY IN SPITE OF DIVISION

Sometimes historians reveal their secular bias by the way they describe the work of Christian missionaries in Africa. They often assume that missionaries were disrespectful of local culture and not able to harmonize their religious message with local traditions. Historians also tend to assume that missionaries worked hand in hand with the colonial officials. Additionally, historians tend to look at the different denominations that have sent out missionaries and conclude that the missionaries created some lasting divisions among the people. None of these perspectives fit the experience of Christian missions in Burundi.

Establishing Christian mission work in Burundi was a hazardous occupation at first. The Society of Missionaries of Our Lady of Africa sent their first missionaries to Burundi in 1879. Their common name, "White Fathers," was not because of their white skins. They had adopted long white robes as the dress for their order, to help them fit in with the Arabs of North Africa, where they first did mission work. The first two White Fathers to come to Burundi survived less than two years before they were killed by local people, probably urged on by Arab slave traders. The Arabs didn't want any interference with their work and felt the sultans' claims on the coast entitled them to a free hand in the interior. Between 1881, when the first missionaries were killed, and 1898, the White Fathers made four more attempts to establish mission work in Burundi, but all these efforts were unsuccessful. This was largely because of the continued opposition of the Arabs and of local people resistant to Christianity and European influence.

Finally in 1898 the White Fathers were able to establish a mission station at Mugera that survived, followed by stations at Muyaga, Buhonga, Kanyinya, Rugari, and Buhoro. The Catholic mission work continued, but there was still considerable opposition. Mwami (King) Gisabo tried to get them out of his territory. German officials, on the other hand, tried to protect them, but were not happy with the fact that the missionaries spoke French and were not submissive to German authority. A major issue that divided the Catholic missionaries and the German officials was the German preference for working with the Tutsis, while the Catholics found the Hutus to be more open to Christianity. (Donald Hohensee, *Church Growth in Burundi,* South Pasadena: William Carey Library, 1977, pp. 37-39)

German authorities in Burundi found greater harmony with the first Protestant missionaries than with the Catholics. The Neukirchner Missionsgesellschaft (German Lutheran) missionaries arrived in 1911. Their use of the German language gave them something in common with the German colonial authorities. Also, German authorities were pleased that the Protestant missionaries were willing to work to evangelize the Tutsis, something the Catholics were reluctant to do. Both Protestants and Catholics devoted much of their attention to establishing schools, with the encouragement of the German officials.

The arrival of the Belgian troops and the quick defeat of the German garrisons had differing impacts on Catholic and Protestant missions. The White Fathers spoke French, as did the Belgians, and Catholicism was dominant in Belgium. Also, the White Fathers were in no way connected with the Germans. So the Belgians not only permitted the White Fathers to continue their work, but also decided to provide funding for mission schools and health facilities. This government sponsorship and funding was restricted to the Catholics for most of the time the Belgians controlled Burundi. The result was the flourishing of Catholicism in the country. At first most Catholics were from the lower classes, but in the 30s and 40s people of all levels converted to the Catholic Church, including many of the local chiefs. By the time of independence in 1962, the Catholic churches counted more than 1.5 million members. (Hohensee, p. 39)

The Protestant missionaries prior to 1916 were Germans and had to leave when the Belgians took over, so there was little to show for their efforts, except for the stones with which their buildings had been built. The first Protestants to enter Burundi after World War I were the Seventh Day Adventists, who in 1925 moved over from their work in Congo. Then in 1928, the Danish Baptist Church and Mission Society sought and received permission from the Belgians to start work in Burundi. They established themselves in 1928 at Musema in the north, at one of the sites where the German Lutherans had worked. By virtue of their standing as the first Protestant mission group approved by the Belgians, the Danish Baptists became the informal clearinghouse for other Protestant mission agencies seeking to begin work in Burundi. First the Friends, then the Free Methodists sought and obtained permission from the Danish Baptists to establish work at former German government stations. The Danish Baptists had concluded that they could not work in all parts of Burundi, so were willing to be joined by other groups that were compatible theologically.

The Friends Africa Gospel Mission came from a desire expressed at Kansas Yearly Meeting of Friends in 1932, to "find an untouched field and open a Mission in Africa." The following year Kansas Yearly Meeting commissioned Arthur and Edna Chilson, experienced Friends missionaries from Kenya, to go west and south from Kenya, looking for opportunities for mission work. They investigated parts of Tanganyika and Congo, and then arrived in Burundi. They were impressed with the large number of people and the very limited Protestant mission work there. The Chilsons made contact with the Danish Baptists in Burundi and requested permission to start work at the former German Protestant station at Kibimba, in the central part of the country.

When the Chilsons were ready to move to Burundi, they thought they could make the trip by automobile and truck from Nairobi to Burundi in five days, but it took three weeks instead. They had lots of trouble with their vehicles and the roads turned out to be much more difficult than they had expected. Edna Chilson described one part of their trip as follows:

> Some of the rivers that we had to cross were not bridged, so we crossed them by ferry. The large platform was sometimes built on pontoons or canoes made from hollowed-out logs. It was quite exciting when the truck, which was rather heavily loaded, put its front wheels on the ferry. It looked for a few moments as if the ferry and all would dip under the water, but, as soon as the other wheels came onto it, things righted themselves. Some of the rivers were wide and rather swift; others not so angry looking. Many of the roads cling to the sides of steep hills and a nervous passenger does not enjoy looking to the depths below. (*Urundi for Christ: A History of the Friends Africa Gospel Mission of Kansas Yearly Meeting, 1933-1940*, Wichita, KS, 1941, pp. 8-9)

After receiving approval from the board of the Danish Baptist Mission to start work in Kibimba, the Chilsons set about to build a residence and a church. They salvaged some of the bricks and stones from the German station and were able to rescue some fruit trees and flowers as well. In short order they were able to move from their tents into a temporary residence. Things went well in getting the mission established, apart from the unpleasant experience of having robbers tunnel under the wall of their house and steal food and clothing.

A year after the Chilsons began the work, Kansas Yearly Meeting appointed the Chilsons' daughter, Esther Chilson Choate, and her husband, Ralph, as the next missionaries. A succession of other missionaries joined them in the coming decades. An intriguing artifact of the life of these early missionaries is a travel trailer brought from the United States by the Choates. It is still parked near my house in Bujumbura and is sometimes used to house staff for the Burundi Yearly Meeting guest house. The early Friends missionaries not only preached the word of God, but also taught the people how to read and write, how to plant trees, and how to pursue various professions. They also treated people with various diseases and taught them about personal hygiene.

Later on, a hospital was built at Kibimba; Dr. Perry Rawson became its first physician, A school was established, called the Arthur Chilson Normal School, in memory of the pioneering missionary work of the Chilsons. Some of the early missionaries have gone on to receive their heavenly rewards, but others are still living. They all deserve great appreciation for their sacrificial ministries.

Near the time the Friends started work in Burundi, other Protestants joined them. These included the World Gospel Mission, the Swedish Pentecostals, and the Anglicans. The potential existed for competition and conflict among the Protestant missions, all seeking to establish work in a relatively small country. Fortunately, instead of competing with one another, most of the Protestant groups joined in forming the Protestant Alliance in 1935. Recognizing they were in the minority in relation to the Catholic Church and that the government favored the Catholics, the Protestant Alliance sought to present a united voice to the government. The Alliance also determined the territories to be assigned to new missions seeking to start work. As a result, the Anglicans concentrated their work in the north and the south, World Gospel Mission in the east, and the Baptists in the northwest. This left the central area to be divided among the Free Methodists and the Friends. These agreements were negotiated on a friendly basis, setting a good example of peaceful cooperation for those who would find Christ and become leaders of the churches in the future.

The Protestant Alliance also became the organizing group for a number of joint projects among all or part of the members of the Alliance, including Mweya Bible School, Central Africa Evangelical Seminary, Grace Memorial Press, Burundi Literature Center, and Radio CORDAC. There were some problems involved with these cooperative projects, but in general they permitted work to be done that could not have been done by any one mission group. Although the Pentecostals, Adventists, and Plymouth Brethren did not join the alliance, this did not prevent the general spirit of cooperation from continuing during the period when the mission groups were at work. (Hohensee, p. 42)

It was in the 1940s that the Great Revival of East Africa took place. Part of the impetus of the revival was a dramatic renewal movement originating in Rwanda and spreading across the border. The Anglicans were active in the revival, leading the way in many confessions of spiritual waywardness on the part of Christians and renewed diligence in Bible study and prayer. One account of the revival in Rwanda shows its intensity:

The Spirit had come amongst them. For two-and-a-half hours men rose, sometimes several at a time, overcome by conviction of sin. There was uncontrolled weeping and crying out, followed by overwhelming joy and burning love. One after another offered to carry the news of the Savior's redemption to the farthest parts of the land. It had suddenly become so glorious, so sweet, that they simply could not keep silent. One by one they set out, to the extreme disruption of school and hospital routine and the intense annoyance of some of the more orderly minded. (Hohensee, p. 91)

The revival spread into Burundi and among the various denominations, with the full support of the Alliance of Protestant Churches. It was clear to everyone involved that God was at work and would not confine His work to certain denominations. Thus the revival became a unifying factor among Christians.

**David, you've talked about revival among the Protestants during the time the missionaries were here and I think you said the Catholic Church was growing very fast during this time as well. How do you explain the rapid adoption of Christianity among the people of Burundi?**

**Well, Emmanuel, you've noticed I've emphasized the theme of unity amid disunity. To the credit of many of the missionaries, they sensed that they need not destroy the culture of Burundi, but set out to show that Christianity could fit with and bring to fruition many of the tradition-al spiritual values. In many other parts of Africa, this transition was not nearly as smooth. Tradition in Burundi was built around one high God, Imana. Rather than attacking this idea as contradictory to Christianity, by and large the missionaries preached about the God of the Bible being consistent with the monotheism of Burundi culture. Burundi culture, like that of much of Africa, features proverbs and parables, conveying deep meanings not understood by all. The missionaries were able to show how the parables and proverbs of the Bible were very sim-ilar. Traditional Burundi religion includes a belief in spirits and the new message of the Christian Gospel featured the work of the Holy Spirit, God's presence to transform and**

empower people today. Traditional Burundi religion in Burundi is not focused on idols and images, so it has been easy for Burundians to understand that the symbols of the church are not idols, but representations of Christian history and Christian truth. The people were not asked to throw away their ideas, but to see them brought to completion by Christianity.

You know, David, what you wrote about the Protestant Alliance made me think about the Berlin Conference and the song about our own chiefs dividing up Burundi. Doesn't it seem like the Protestant Alliance carved up Burundi just like the Europeans carved up Africa?

Well, Emmanuel, I can see why you would say that. Actually, I don't think that was the case. My sense from reading about the history of missions here is that the Protestant Alliance simply provided a structure for the cooperation that came about as the Danish Baptists welcomed other like-minded Protestant missions to join them in Burundi. None of these groups had unlimited personnel and resources. By agreeing that they would work in different areas instead of competing in the same localities, they were able to enhance the spread of the Gospel and set a good example for Burundi Christians by working together in love and mutual respect. At least I see it as a force for unity in our country rather than some kind of Christian colonialism.

I can see what you're saying about unity coming from the transition from traditional religion to Christianity. But aren't Catholicism and Protestantism fundamentally different from one another and wasn't there an inevitable clash between them?

That's been true in some places, Emmanuel. Even though Catholics and Protestants established separate churches, schools, and hospitals, there hasn't been hatred and conflict between them in Burundi. I think it might have to do with the kinds of missionaries that came to Burundi and the relatively recent introduction of Christianity in Burundi. By and large, the Catholics have been true to the Bible and to the basics of Christianity. In some other places, local traditions and beliefs have gotten mixed into their worship and their doctrine. In Burundi we have been blessed with a Christian movement that is relatively sound theologically, and there is a considerable amount of agreement among Christians about their faith.

David, if Christians have been living in harmony in Burundi, then how do you explain all the violence in the last few decades?

Oh, that's another matter, Emmanuel. I didn't say Christians were all being faithful to love each other and forgive their enemies. Unfortunately, that's not been the case. It's definitely the case that Christians, or at least those who identify themselves as Christians—Protestants and Catholics—have been involved in the killings. We'll have to tackle that subject another day.

David, did you say it was during your father's lifetime that the first Friends missionaries arrived to work in Burundi?

Yes, Emmanuel. Let me tell you a little more about my father and his memories of the arrival of the missionaries. First of all, I should tell you about the recovery of my father from terrible illness. I wouldn't be here to tell you the story if God hadn't spared his life when he was a child.

My father had four brothers. They had everything they needed: milk, meat, beans, peas, potatoes, bananas, cassava, etc. There were also many people who worked in their gardens and benefited from their abundant crops. Then a disease struck all the children. Since there were no hospitals in those days, his father called for the witchdoctors or traditional healers to help. Everyone in the village believed that the children were bewitched. Before the healers could do anything to treat them, his brothers began dying. The witchdoctors felt helpless, as they could not even identify the children's sickness. They called the ailment "rashes." Today we would call it in English, "chicken pox."

All my father's brothers died and everyone was expecting my father to die as well. He was very sick and was placed in a hut alone so others wouldn't be infected. People sat outside the hut, ready to come and pick him up for burial. He could hear them whispering, "Has he passed away?" "No, he is still breathing," was the reply. Amazingly, my father clung to his life. Finally, he got well, recovered and woke up. Because of the terrible scars from the chicken pox on his body, they named him Bikomagu, which means "marks." In those days, those who became Christians were given a "Christian" name, often from the Bible, to go with their given name. In my father's case his nickname "Bikomagu" was converted to English and he was called "Mark."

When my father was about nine years old, he saw something very unusual on the hill overlooking his village. Things which looked like cows suddenly appeared on the hill not far from his home. The next day the "cows" were still there, and they were still there after a week. He and some other boys in the village decided to go and see why the cows were not moving. Just as Moses decided to approach the burning bush to see why it was not being consumed, the children fearfully climbed the hill. When they got close enough to see more clearly, to their amazement, the "cows" were actually small tents that the first missionaries had pitched on the hill. Of course the boys had never seen tents before. All they could think of was that these were some form of clothing. Now, the boys did not have any clothes on, which was typical in those days. Only adults wore clothing and that was just a small piece of material made from the bark of a tree.

As the boys got nearer to the tents, they discovered that there were white people living in that "clothing"! These fascinating white people were Arthur and Edna Chilson and their daughter Rachel, who had just arrived as the first Friends missionaries in Burundi. It was Rachel who attracted the boys' attention, for she was bouncing a tennis ball, something the boys had never seen before. The boys tried to speak to the Chilsons, but they spoke Kiswahili, which they had learned in Kenya. Kirundi and Swahili are not drastically different, but these boys realized it would take some effort to get to know this white girl and her family. The Chilsons played a record for the children, with songs on it. The children were fascinated with the record player, but still could not understand the words.

The Chilsons quickly learned Kirundi, even though there were no Kirundi books at the time. My father and the other boys of the village helped the missionaries with their first building, by bringing sand to exchange for salt. My father was one of the first to accept the Lord as his personal Savior in response to Arthur Chilson's preaching. I remember my father telling me about Mr. Chilson's sermon about the resurrection of Jesus and the scars of the nails on His hands. This made my father think about his own scars from chicken pox and of his own "resurrection" as a small boy. It was in 1956 when he became one of the first Friends ministers after attending the Mweya Bible Institute and then became superintendent of the churches.

**How about you, David? Did you become a Christian as a result of the missionaries' work?**


**When I was born in 1959, I grew up in a Christian home and I had a very good faith foundation, thanks to the work of the missionaries and the influence of my godly parents.**

Of course, I needed to make my own commitment to Christ, which I did in 1976. I asked Jesus to come into my life and forgive my sins. But I had learned about Christ from an early age. As a small boy, I liked the stories we learned in the Sunday School and VBS classes. By the time I became a teenager, I enjoyed memorizing the Bible, singing in the church choir, and attending youth camps. We have the missionaries to thank for those programs.

"Forgiveness is the fragrance
the violet sheds on the heel
that has crushed it."

                    -Mark Twain

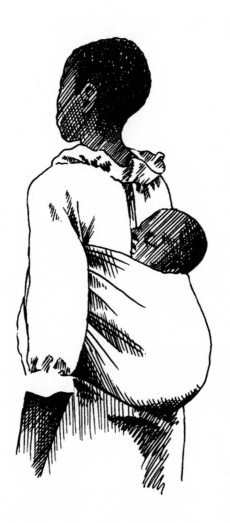

# 6

# THREE DECADES OF TRAGEDY

The year I was born, in 1959, was an active time in the birth of nationalism in Burundi. That year Prince Louis Rwagasore, eldest son of King Mwambutsa IV, married Marie-Rose Ntamikevyo, a young Hutu woman. The marriage was calculated to strengthen his support among the Hutu majority. Rwagasore was not only the prince, but was also the leader of the strongest nationalist political party, the Union Pour le Progres National (UPRONA). Like the other European powers with African colonies, the Belgians had responded to local unrest and nationalism by allowing limited opportunities for democracy. UPRONA's major competitor was the Parti Democrate Chretien (PDC), supported by the Belgian government as a more moderate alternative to UPRONA, in the hope of delaying the push for independence.

In legislative elections in 1961, Rwagasore's party won 80 percent of the votes cast and secured 58 of the 80 seats in the legislative assembly. However, before Rwagasore could take office as prime minister, he was assassinated by a Greek man, from all indications employed by leaders of the rival party, the CDP. Like the assassination of the president of the United States, John F. Kennedy, two years later, the loss of Rwagasore was a serious blow to the emerging democracy in Burundi. He was young, charismatic, capable, and he had built his political support among both ethnic groups. The loss of his leadership potential and the anger generated within UPRONA had much to do with the sad events that followed. (Lemarchand, pp. 53-57)

Whether or not the Belgians engineered Rwagasore's assassination, this was a terrible thing to happen on the eve of independence. Of course the Belgians had not invented strife and rivalry in Burundi. As we have seen, the roots of both conflict and reconciliation reached far back into the history of Burundi. But a number of Belgium's colonial policies had disturbed existing systems of governance and had helped set local leaders against one another. For example, in the early 1930s the Belgians consolidated numerous independent chiefdoms under a small number of powerful Ganwa. This disenfranchised a number of Tutsi chiefs and the number of Hutu chiefs was drastically reduced. To the Belgians, the new system was more efficient administratively, but to the Burundi leaders it was a disaster. Not only did the new system make it easier for the Belgians to increase their demands for taxes and forced labor, it threw the historic distribution of power into disarray. (Lemarchand, p. 43)

Meanwhile, as events moved closer to independence, ethnic violence had escalated in neighboring Rwanda, with a different set of dynamics than in Burundi. A Hutu uprising began there in 1959, partially in response to the brutal beating of a Hutu leader by Tutsis, followed by revenge attacks on Tutsis by Hutus. Thousands of Tutsis were killed, with many others fleeing across the border into Burundi. Burundi and Rwanda are separate entities with all sorts of political and social differences, but their proximity and their identical ethnic makeup means that turmoil in one country frequently spills over into the other.

Beginning with the Gold Coast (Ghana) gaining its independence from Britain in 1957, European colonies in Africa moved steadily toward independence. There were some reasons for optimism about the prospects for a peaceful transition to independence in Burundi. For a number of years,

Burundians had participated in political parties. The election in 1961 had been peaceful, at least prior to the assassination of Rwagasore. And the Belgians had enough respect for tradition to retain the monarchy, under King Mwambutsa IV, as a constitutional monarchy, with a prime minister sharing power with the king. Moreover, a serious effort was made to balance the numbers of Hutus and Tutsi in the new government.

The hopeful aspects of the achievement of independence in 1962 were marred by the bitterness over Rwagasore's death a few months before and the loss of his potentially strong leadership. He definitely would have been prime minister and he had at least a strong possibility of leading the country effectively, balancing the distinct perspectives of the ethnic groups and the other rivalries from the past. No one of Rwagasore's caliber was found to serve as prime minister in the early years of independence. After several persons served ineffectively as prime minister, King Mwambutsa called on Pierre Ngendandumwe, formerly a close associate of Rwagasore and a Hutu, to form a new government.

Burundi's young history repeated itself in 1965 as the establishment of a new government gave way to hatred and murder. Three days after Prime Minister Ngendandumwe took office and on the day he announced his new cabinet, assassins shot and killed him. Although it was difficult to determine responsibility for the killing at the time, apparently the killers were Rwandese Tutsi refugees, trying to prevent a Hutu from becoming the head of Burundi's government. Until that time, there had been a reasonable balance of opportunities for Hutus and Tutsi in Burundi. The ethnic divide had not been as sharp as in Rwanda.

The trend toward ethnically dominated politics accelerated during the next elections in October 1965. The UPRONA party won three-quarters of the seats in the national assembly and a substantial majority of the UPRONA and independent candidates were Hutu. Nevertheless, King Mwambutsa appointed his personal secretary, Leopold Biha, a Tutsi, as prime minister. Hutu politicians felt one of their group should have become prime minister. Not only that, but he lacked the experience to lead the country. (Gerard Prunier, *"Burundi: Descent Into Chaos or a Manageable Crisis?"* Writenet Country Paper, www.unhcr.ch/refworld/country/writenet/wribdi01.htm.)

In the coming days, events quickly went from bad to worse, and continued to spiral into more Hutu-Tutsi violence. One of the Hutu political leaders who himself had hoped to be prime minister, led a coup attempt that not only had as its goal the elimination of the prime minister, but the king as well. The coup quickly failed, but it led to ethnic fighting which claimed both Tutsi and Hutu victims. One of the army officers who had defeated the unsuccessful coup attempt was Captain Michel Micombero. His role in restoring order won him the support of other Tutsi officers who agreed that a new kind of government should be established in Burundi, with the power to be monopolized by the Tutsi.

To establish control over the government, Micombero and his allies deposed King Mwambutsa in mid-1966 and replaced him with his son, Prince Ndizeye, who took the name of Ntare V. Micombero then named himself prime minister and a few months later abolished the monarchy. It was bad enough that Micombero did away with both democracy and the monarchy in a matter of months. But the more ominous changes occurred in the composition of his military dictatorship. Micombero appointed other Tutsi extremists to key positions, forced most Hutus out of the government, and sidelined the remnants of the Ganwa elite. All that remained in national politics was a racially dominated government, determined to have its way. One of the last Hutu military officers, Commander Martin Ndayahoze, said of the new politics of race: "Greedy politicians use ethnic divisiveness as a political strategy. So if they are Tutsi, they denounce a 'Hutu peril' which must be fought, even by violence. And if they are Hutu they clamor against a 'Tutsi apartheid,' which must be ended." (Prunier, p. 5)

## MORE TRAGEDIES IN 1972

Military dictatorships were common in Africa in the 1970s as the newly independent countries struggled to create a post-independence political culture that could survive internal divisions. Some of these African countries were fractured into all sorts of ethnic and political divisions. Burundi did not have a history of deep ethnic divisions, but Micombero managed to cultivate hatred and fear across the ethnic lines where there had been cooperation and coexistence in the past. Not only did he alienate most Hutus, who no longer had a voice in government, but he also angered significant numbers of the other Tutsis. Those who were loyal to the monarchy were bitter about the abrupt ending of King Ntare's reign. Tutsi politicians who had seen their power wane during the Micombero regime were also bitter.

The Tutsi and Hutu opponents of Micombero did not have a lot in common, but they agreed to give support to King Ntare V in restoring the monarchy. Unfortunately for this restoration effort, Micombero, who had agreed to allow Ntare to return to Burundi in March 1972, had him arrested when he arrived. The Tutsis and Hutus who had supported Ntare's return then attempted to launch an uprising. But Micombero had Ntare killed and ordered his supporters to begin retribution on the Hutu, overlooking the part his Tutsi rivals had in the attempt to restore the throne. State security and army teams started with the targeting of Micombero's political rivals, then quickly moved on to seeking out and killing Hutu leaders with no particular political involvement. The killers reasoned that they might expect leadership and resistance from educated Hutus, so they set out to locate and kill them.

It is very difficult to describe the events of 1972 in an objective, dispassionate way. For example, wildly different estimates of the numbers of casualties circulated at the time and it still cannot be determined how many victims there were. Considering that Burundi's population at the time was under four million, by anyone's estimate, the consequences of the violence were enormous. And the impact of the deaths was even greater because of the targeting of educated Hutus. Micombero succeeded in intimidating his enemies for a time, but descended into depression and heavy drinking, perhaps scarred deep inside by the awfulness of the massacre he had ordered.

Colonel Jean-Baptiste Bagaza, from the same part of Burundi as Micombero, forced him from office in 1976. Some were hopeful about the change of government for a time, but Bagaza's regime ended up following many of the ways of the Micombero government. Tutsis kept control of most government positions, were given most teaching jobs, and most of the admissions to the university. Not only were the Hutus shut out, but the Tutsis not from Bagaza's own lineage could not expect to gain significant positions in the government. The politics of paranoia extended to the ordinary people, who were arrested for the slightest offence. Bagaza's people harassed officials of the Catholic Church for objecting to the elimination of almost all civil liberties. Before a group of army officers forced Bagaza to step down in 1987, his officials had even begun detaining Tutsi leaders he didn't trust.

The third in the series of army officers to head the government in Burundi was Major Pierre Buyoya, who was from the same area as Micombero and Bagaza. And like the previous governments, his was overwhelmingly made up of Tutsis. But Buyoya set about to reform the repressive system of government, which had become increasingly harsh for the nearly twenty years of military rule. There was a relatively minor episode of violence in 1987, at least by comparison with the bloodshed in 1972. The violence started with an episode in which Hutu peasants began killing Tutsi. In response, the army killed any Hutu they could find, guilty or not, particularly in the Ntega and Marangara communes in northern Burundi. Ironically, Hutu and Tutsi extremists feared the possibility of a change in the status quo for different reasons. The Tutsi

extremists wanted to continue a regime built on ethnically ori-
ented politics and the Hutu extremists feared their following
would be lost if there was significant reform in the government.

In spite of or maybe because of these events in 1987,
Buyoya took significant steps to restore democracy and opportunities for the Hutu. He named Adrien Sibomana as premier,
the first Hutu to fill this position in more than twenty years. He
appointed a commission to study the problems of national disunity. He allowed a group of Hutus to organize a new political
party, Front pour la Democratie au Burundi (FRODEBU). To
assure there would be a multiparty system, he set about re-
organizing UPRONA, giving leadership positions to both Hutu
and Tutsi persons. Buyoya opened the civil service, the
schools, and the university to Hutus, although he didn't try to
end the Tutsi dominance of the army.

## STILL MORE TRAGEDIES IN 1993

The restoration of democracy seemed to be in good order
during most of 1993. With Buyoya's encouragement, voters
adopted a new constitution in 1992, which prescribed the
basis for national elections. Buyoya ran for president as
UPRONA's candidate, but he lost the race to FRODEBU's candidate, Melchior Ndadaye, in an orderly and honest election.
In the subsequent legislative election, FRODEBU candidates
again outpolled UPRONA candidates two to one. The successful candidates in both parties included both Hutus and
Tutsis.

The elections were hopeful to those who wanted to see a
change in the status quo, but not everyone did. Extremist
Tutsis in the army launched a coup attempt a few days after
the legislative election, but it was not successful. Many of the
FRODEBU supporters who received posts in the new government were inexperienced, since Hutus had been shut out of
the government for so long and things did not go smoothly in

the transition. Radical Hutus objected to the ethnic balance in Ndadaye's cabinet and radical Tutsis were fearful of his plans to encourage refugees to return.

As a first step in their plan to take over the government, on October 20 a particular unit of the army set in motion an attack on the Presidential Palace. Army personnel drove President Ndadaye to an army camp, assuring him he would be safe there, but the coup leaders killed him the next day, along with many other officials in his government. The leadership of the coup collapsed in short order, but there was a period of chaos before the remnants of the Ndadaye government were able to reorganize and resume leadership.

Anger over the assassination of Ndadaye, disappointment over the electoral defeat of UPRONA, and the desire of both Tutsi and Hutu extremists that the FRODEBU government not be reconstructed all produced a new cauldron of violence. Hutu radicals began killing Tutsis soon after the assassination. The army responded to these killings with its own widespread killings of Hutus. In later stages of the violence, Hutu extremists killed Hutus who had not supported FRODEBU, blaming UPRONA for the failed coup. The army began protecting Tutsis and then went back to killing Hutus. The death toll from these killings was as hard to estimate as it had been in 1972, but could have been higher than in 1972 and it continued through the nineties.

President Ndadaye's successor, Cyprien Ntaryamira, a Hutu, had almost no time to restore political stability and democracy. Within two months after he took office, he was killed when the airplane he was riding in was shot down. Another passenger in the plane was President Habyarimana of Rwanda. Massive killing occurred in Rwanda after the plane crash, but not so in Burundi. In mid-July 1996, former president Pierre Buyoya organized a successful coup and took over as president.

David, I've read about some of this history, but I've also heard you talk a little about how the violence impacted you and your family and I'd like you to tell me a little more about that. I know some of it is painful to talk about, but there are also some wonderful stories of people giving witness to God's grace as they lost their lives.

You're right about that, Emmanuel. God has been good during some terrible times. You remember that in the 1972 killings it was the well-educated persons who were the most vulnerable to attack. Abel Binyoni, a headmaster at Kwibuka primary school, was one of the leaders to be apprehended and taken away for execution. He was known as a very godly man and a wonderful singer. Very little is known about many of the killings, but in this case one of the soldiers was also a follower of Christ and later told about the details of his death. Knowing he was about to be killed, Binyoni asked if he could sing a song. When the soldiers reluctantly granted his request, he lifted his tenor voice and sang, "Jesus I come." One of the lines in the song was particularly appropriate, "Out of earth's sorrows into Thy balm, out of life's storm and into Thy calm, out of distress to jubilant psalm, Jesus, I come to Thee." My father was a close friend of Abel and was very distressed by his death.

At about the same time as Binyoni was killed, my father received the disturbing news that my brother Joel had been murdered at the Kiremba High School. Joel lost his life because he remained at the compound trying to comfort a group of young students in a Scripture Union group, of which he was the leader.

Meanwhile, some Hutus called for the killing of Tutsis, blaming them for the crisis. Some Tutsis, with the assistance of soldiers, carried out revenge by killing Hutus, as in the case of the Kwibuka massacre described in the first chapter.

David, didn't you once say that your father-in-law was killed in this violence?

Yes he was, Emmanuel. He was killed by villagers in the Giheta area simply because he was Tutsi. Alphonse, my brother-in-law, had been warned by his friend that armed men were searching for his father. Having been born in a mixed family, my father-in-law did not believe that his neighbors would kill him simply because he was a Tutsi. He did not run away and he probably died with no idea what his murderers were about to do.

In some parts of the country people had to participate in a massive hide-and-seek game, which of course was not a game at all. I have heard testimonies of Hutu people hiding Tutsis and vice versa, in different parts of the country. It is because of such acts of love and courage that we believe that people on both sides can contribute to the promotion of peace and reconciliation.

Chantal, my sister-in-law, was a student in one of the high schools in the Gitega area. Gitega is the second largest city of Burundi and has the greatest number of high schools outside Bujumbura. In one school the situation had become so terrible the students themselves killed their headmaster, his wife and children. At Chantal's school, during the tense days after the death of President Ndadaye, students divided themselves into two groups according to their ethnic identity. She and another girl decided they did not want to be identified with either group. In Chantal's case, she probably thought that identifying with one of the ethnic groups would have meant disappointing one of her parents, since they were from the two different groups. When the solders came to her school, they saw Chantal was not with the other students, so they wrongly assumed she had organized the separating of the students into the two groups. After the soldiers attacked her and she was taken to the hospital, the last word she said before she died was that she wanted a nurse to clean the blood from her body, so she might present herself to Jesus in a pure state.

David, you tell these stories so matter of factly. Don't you and Felicity feel angry about all these tragic deaths?

Well, Emmanuel, we probably have felt that way at times. It all seemed so pointless. But remember what I told you about God's deliverance from bitterness and how God taught me to forgive the killers of my students at Kwibuka. The same God has given an extra measure of grace to Felicity and me in dealing with the deaths of our loved ones.

"To be a Christian

means to forgive the inexcusable,

because God has forgiven

the inexcusable in you."

-C.S. Lewis

# 7

# THE IMPACT OF VIOLENCE ON THE CHRISTIAN CHURCH

Burundi has one of the highest percentages of Christians in the world. It is commonly estimated that 65 percent of the people of Burundi are Catholic, 25 percent are Protestant, 5 percent are Moslems, and the remaining 5 percent are those who still adhere to the old traditional religion or simply do not worship anywhere. This raises numerous questions, especially in the light of the terrible civil war that has scarred the country for years. With such a large number of Christians in Burundi, it seems fair to ask what Gospel these Christians have been preaching? Can it be only the small number of non-Christians who are causing the terror and the desolation of the whole country? What impact has the Gospel made on the lives of Christians? To the last question, Antoine Rutayisire, leader of the African Evangelistic Enterprise of Rwanda, gave the following answer:

> Unfortunately, we remember what we could have done better when it is too late, when the tragedy is consumed, when the situation is irreversible! But maybe this question might not be useless...so that the church which is operating in the tense situation of ethnic, tribal, racial, and others may adapt its methodology of presenting the Gospel in an effective and preventive way. (Antoine Rutayisire, *Faith Under Fire,* African Enterprise)

In the early sixties, missionaries still provided much of the leadership of the church in Burundi. The Belgians quickly dismantled their colonial system, but the European and American missionaries stayed on. This was not bad. They gave of themselves selflessly in service to Christ and worked to train Burundians for leadership of the churches, the schools, and the other Christian enterprises. As they saw the difficulties in the transition from European to Burundian control of the government, they began to look toward the day when Burundians would completely lead the church.

Missionaries were not in immediate danger in Burundi in the early 1960s. But they were conscious of the hazards created by political turmoil. They knew about problems in neighboring countries, particularly the killing of nineteen Catholic missionaries in the turmoil in Congo in 1964. Friends missionaries were startled by the abrupt deportation of one of the Friends couples, Randall and Sara Brown. Randall had grown up in Burundi with his missionary parents, Clayton and Louella Brown. Randall had been director of the Friends secondary school in Kibimba when the Hutu and Tutsi students became more and more uneasy about their coexistence in the school. He tried to calm the situation by agreeing to sleep in the dormitory with the male students to prevent trouble arising, but conflict continued and he closed the school. Apparently the local governor heard from persons who were disgruntled about the school, so he decided to request that his superiors initiate the deportation.

The Browns' deportation, the same year as the first serious ethnic and political conflict erupted, was an effect, rather than a cause of the increasing tension. Missionaries in general were not implicated in the political and ethnic tension. They had worked very hard to minister the Gospel to people of any ethnic background. They were conscious of being guests in the country and worked hard not to show favoritism toward any group or faction. Some of the missions were located in areas where almost all the church attenders and students were Hutu, but this reflected the demographics of their areas, not a plan to exclude Tutsis.

Looking back on the violent events that began in 1965, one might wonder if the missionaries and the Burundian pastors and teachers could have done more to teach and preach about love, forgiveness, and reconciliation. First of all, to ask such a question presumes that one could have predicted the violence that engulfed the country soon after independence and this was simply not possible. The missionaries sought to preach and teach the Gospel of Christ, which is centered in the love of God and of all persons. They did not shy away from Christ's teaching about loving our enemies. But any teaching that would have been aimed specifically at ethnic and political conflict would probably have been inappropriate and ineffective if initiated by missionaries.

As for intervening directly to protect Burundians who were in danger, I have talked with missionaries about the anguish they felt over their precarious circumstances. They knew and loved many of those who were apprehended and taken away. One missionary spoke of watching people being led away with bayonets in their backs and never seeing them again. In some cases, I'm told, the missionaries gave shelter to those in danger, at considerable risk. But in general the missionaries reacted about the way the Burundian victims did, not knowing what to do, realizing that resistance by force was both futile and contrary to Christ's teaching.

Even though the American missionaries were not directly involved in the conflict and did not speak out regarding the political turmoil, American officials were still concerned for the missionaries' safety. The U.S. ambassador during the 1972 crisis, Thomas Melady, took steps to assure the safety of American missionaries. Melady was Catholic, but he was primarily dealing with the safety of the Protestant missionaries, since most of the Catholic mission workers were European. Melady noted with concern that an army unit searched the Seventh Day Adventist mission station near Bujumbura. His fear was that the government might be trying to make a case that missionaries were involved in the Hutu side of the struggle. Melady met with President Micombero and urged him to restrain his officials and army troops from attacking American citizens. Melady was able to strengthen his statements of concern by promising substantial American funds for food, medical supplies, and blankets for displaced persons. (Thomas Patrick Melady, *Burundi: The Tragic Years*, New York: Orbis Books, 1974, pp. 8-10)

In spite of the efforts of American officials, the Burundi government proceeded to deport a number of missionaries and to deny visa renewals to most of the rest. One of the deported couples, James and Doris Morris, Friends missionaries from Kansas, were in Kenya in 1979 for medical attention. The U.S. ambassador to Burundi relayed word to his counterpart in Kenya that the Morrises would not be allowed to return. Later they were given permission to go back to Burundi and collect what they could of their belongings, but they only had forty-eight hours to deal with all of this. They recall with sadness the steady flow of people to their house to say goodbye to them. They say it was very much like the way people acted when there was a death in the family. The people said very little, expressing their love and respect by simply sitting with them.

Certainly no one would invite and welcome trouble as a means of strengthening the faith of Christian believers. There was nothing good about the violence that began in 1965. But there were some good results, especially in the spiritual strengthening of those who experienced the brutalities and survived. The testimony of a believer in Rwanda is typical of those of many of the victims: "While they were beating me over the head, I felt the Lord Jesus to be very near to me. I felt Him in a way as never before. I thank God for that time in prison because it made the Lord more real to me. Now I want to serve Him." (Norman A. Wingert, *No Place to Stop Killing*, Chicago: Moody Press, 1974, p. 93)

The loss of many leaders in 1972 was terrible, but God certainly did not abandon those who trusted in Him. A previous generation had experienced the Great Revival of East Africa. In the midst of the violence of the seventies, people began turning to God, their only source of hope and strength. Revival exploded among the youth, especially from 1978 to 1980. I was a participant in a Scripture Union youth camp in 1978, attended by prayer group leaders from various secondary and high schools. There was much confessing, praying, and praising God among the youth who attended. After the camp, the participants took this spirit of revival with them to their schools, churches, and homes. My friends and I went to a number of the schools in the Gitega area, giving our testimonies, preaching, and singing. God used us to bring conviction to people and many of them repented of their sins and accepted Jesus as their Lord and Savior.

Many of today's church leaders in Burundi are a fruit of this revival. The churches in Burundi experienced another new burst of energy in the early 1990s.

Most importantly, God raised up new leaders to take the place of those who were dead and God raised up Burundians with gifts for leadership as the missionaries began to realize their days in our country were numbered.

When the politico-ethnic crisis of 1993 erupted, many people were surprised and disappointed by the way in which the Burundi church passively observed the horrible events. The International Bible Society edited a small booklet called "Where Have the People of God Gone?" In the light of all that took place, some might have even wondered if there were people of God at all in Burundi. During one of the visits of former South African President Nelson Mandela, he went to a Burundi prison. After the visit, he reported to the religious leaders at Gitega that after seeing conditions in the prison, he also wondered if there were any people of God in the country.

David, those are some pretty harsh words about believers in Burundi. Do you think it's fair to say that we Christians in Burundi have been passive and helpless during the past years of violence?

Well, Emmanuel, some of us have done a few things, but I think we have to be honest and own up to the fact that we have not done nearly enough. I think the principal reason for inactivity is fear. I understand fear. I've felt my own life and the lives of my family to be in danger. But I think it unfortunately is the case that some Christians in my country have been so overwhelmed by fear that they have not been able and willing to stand for the truth. There is a saying in Kirundi, "Ubwoba bunyaga ubugabo" (Fear steals away a person's willingness to resist evil). It is as if we put love and fear on a scale, and fear is heavier than love. There are people today who are afraid to say the right thing to those whom they call the wrong people, or to do the right thing at what they call the wrong time. There are no wrong people. Every individual is created in the image of God. And there is no such thing as the wrong time for a Christian to be obedient to God, whatever the consequences. Every time is an opportunity to do good. We must confess the times that we have let fear keep us from acting. We must let love for God and others overcome the fear that grips us. As Solomon said in the Song of Songs 2:5: "Strengthen me with raisins, refresh me with apples, for I am faint with love."

David, aren't there times when Christians have to be concerned about their own lives and their own loved ones?

By all means, Emmanuel. There is no particular virtue in trying to be a martyr. But let me tell you that some Christians in Burundi have acted selfishly. There are those who have looked at the material things they would get if a leader they supported rose to a position of power. Some have supported oppressive leaders so that they might have access to material riches. And yet we Christians know what John says in I John 2:17: "The world and its desires pass away, but the man who does the will of God lives forever." Maybe we are behaving selfishly when, for example, we refuse to give advice to a brother or sister for fear that we might lose our friendship with him/her.

Emmanuel, there is another attitude that has hindered the effectiveness of Christians, namely indifference. I am sure that God is shocked by some Christians' indifference toward the widespread hatred and violence in Burundi in this generation. This is why James says in 4:17 that "Anyone, then, who knows the good he ought to do and doesn't do it, sins." This indifference has caused our people to have an incomplete faith, in the sense that, for them, what is abnormal has become normal! Some Christian parents have not stopped their children from taking up arms to seek revenge.

David, you were born before most of the violence of recent years. My friends and I weren't even born yet when the problems happened in 1972, but we saw our share during 1993. Isn't it the case that most people today are fatalistic about the situation in the country? They talk about the need for peace, but have little hope that it will come about. I've heard that in 1972, many of the victims did nothing to flee or resist the danger. It was good that they were trusting God and were ready to go to heaven. But it seems so wrong to sit idly by and let things continue on.

Oh, Emmanuel, you are so right. But doing something wrong is not better than doing nothing. Taking up arms and simply perpetuating violence is not the answer. We must learn to be wise. We must turn our fatalism into creative efforts to counter violence. Christians must be the leaders in reconciliation and forgiveness, refusing to believe the myth that violence is inevitable. It's true that there have been many wars throughout human history. But it's also true that there have been effective steps taken to end violence. A generation ago, almost no one believed there could be an improvement in the terrible apartheid in South Africa and the violent measures being taken against it. But now we see South Africa as a place of hope. We see it as a place where Christians have been in the forefront of seeking reconciliation and giving forgiveness. If this can happen in such a place of hatred and anger as that, could it not come about in Burundi?

"But genuine forgiveness is participation, reunion overcoming the powers of estrangement. And only because this is so, does forgiveness make love possible. We cannot love unless we have accepted forgiveness, and the deeper our experience of forgiveness is, the greater is our love."

–Paul Tillich

# 8

# THE RELEVANCE OF BIBLICAL TEACHING TO RECONCILIATION

What has gone wrong in this Christian country of mine? What about the large number of conversions that are reported from time to time? Are these masses of people I see walking to and from Sunday services being discipled with good programs that aim to bring about a change of character in their everyday life? Are these people on their way to prayer gatherings intending to pray for wisdom and courage in applying their faith to the issues of violence in our country? Are they praying for grace to break away from the deeply entrenched fear and hatred between Hutus and Tutsis?

Of course I cannot see inside people's hearts and souls to answer these questions. But if I were to be given the chance to speak to all the people of Burundi at once, I would call on them to examine their own attitudes and behavior based on the Scripture that is central to the faith of the Christian majority in our country. Rather than try to discuss the entire Bible, I would focus on a short, but very powerful book, the book of James. In this book I find so many important teachings that relate very closely to the needs in my country.

## FAITH REQUIRES ACTION

The book of James teaches an important spiritual truth, that faith is made complete by actions. It is not enough to be part of a church, have a Christian name, or attend a Sunday Service or Mass. People who are religious but are spiritually dead are like those who look in a mirror and immediately forget what they look like, says James. Their worship and their study of the Bible yields information and inspiration, but no change in their lives. Such people deceive themselves and their religion is worthless, says the writer of James (James 1:26).

The book of James goes on to show the emptiness of faith claims if there are no actions that give evidence of the faith. "Suppose a brother or sister is without clothes and daily food. If one of you says to him, 'Go, I wish you well; keep warm and well fed,' but does nothing about his physical needs, what good is it? In the same way, faith by itself, if it is not accompanied by action, is dead." (James 2:15-17) One might apply this passage to the need to relieve physical hunger in our country, but even more important to our country is the need for people to put their faith into action with respect to love and forgiveness.

To illustrate how faith and actions are linked, James picked Abraham as an example of one of the most important figures in Hebrew history. It was Abraham's willingness to offer his son Isaac as a sacrifice that showed the depth of his faith in God, much more than words could ever have done. James 2:22 says: "You see that his faith and his actions were working together, and his faith was made complete by what he did." It is as if James was telling them this: If Abraham, the friend of God, needed both faith and actions, who are you to say that faith alone is sufficient?

The example of Rahab in the following verses is also powerful. James tells his audience that Rahab the prostitute, a person with a bad reputation, became a prominent woman among the heroes of our faith and she was described as righteous because of giving lodging to the strangers. What an amazing pair of examples used by James: the great father of the Hebrew nation and the lowliest of persons, whose courage and obedience transformed her from the scum of the earth to a person of honor in God's kingdom.

This teaching in the book of James was consistent with Jesus' teaching. In the Sermon on the Mount, Jesus talked about wise and foolish builders. The foolish ones built their house on the sand. They heard Jesus' words, but failed to put them into action. The wise builders constructed their house on the rock, for they not only experienced a transformation of heart, but put their faith into practice (Matthew 7:24-27). Jesus also said in John 15:14 that we are His friends if we do what He commands us. There is much in the Old Testament that also fits with this emphasis on faith and works being inseparable. For example, Proverbs 21:13: "If a man shuts his ears to the cry of the poor, he too will cry out and not be answered."

In Hebrews 11:1 we learn that "faith is being sure of what we hope for and certain of what we do not see." We would expect that this type of faith would be evidenced by prayer, worship, and service to God. What is wrong with this? This is a one-sided approach. It is an incomplete faith. It lacks the other dimension—our relationships with others. If one has a relationship with God, he/she must have a relationship with his or her neighbor also. This is the other dimension, the fellowship with one another, as John calls it. In this fellowship we find the actions that make the faith complete. When you draw a picture of a cross, you cannot just draw a vertical line and call that a cross. It is only a post or a tree without branches. To draw a cross, you must show a horizontal line crossing the vertical line to make the picture of a cross complete.

It is by making a horizontal outreach that we engage in fellowship with one another. The best way to do this is through loving actions. This is how God intended it to be among the human beings and Himself. It is a triangle made up of God, my neighbor, and myself. In Burundian villages many people make a fire between three stones and place a clay pot on them for cooking their food. I have never heard of anyone being able to cook on only two stones. In fact it is dangerous, because if you manage to warm the water on the two stones, by the time the water boils, the pot will get agitated, fall down and burns whoever is near. A faith that only exists between you and your God, like a pot on only two stones, is an incomplete faith.

Cain tried to challenge God by reversing the way God had designed the relationship between those He created. When God, in Genesis 4:9, asked Cain where his brother was Cain replied: "Am I my brother's keeper?" How could Cain have failed to grasp that loving God is only possible if we love others? The relationship God has designed is that we all must be the keepers of our brothers and sisters. Unfortunately, the people of Burundi today still ask Cain's foolish questions. Am I that stranger's "keeper"? Am I the feeder of that hungry person? Am I the provider for the poor people? Am I those fighters' peacemaker? The answers are, "Yes, by all means."

To be one another's keeper is to act in ways that complete our faith. This is what I call living the faith practically. It is living a life of serving one another, as Paul admonished us in Philippians 2:4 "Each of you should look not only to your own interests, but also to the interests of others." The actions of love transcend ethnic, tribal, racial, and national backgrounds and boundaries. C.S. Lewis said that in his day pride was the sin that was more prevalent than any other. I think the greatest sin for Christians today is indifference. It is indifference that causes Christians not to pray. It is indifference that causes Christians not to give. It is indifference that causes Christians not to speak out and denounce evil. And it is indifference that causes those who call themselves Christians not to act against ethnic discrimination and injustice even when they can.

Let us bring our faith to completion by acting in love. Paul said in Romans 12:10. "Be devoted to one another in brotherly love. Honor one another above yourselves." It is through love that we see the wrong person as the right person. Through love, we see impossibility as possibility. Through love, we see the unachievable as the achievable. With love, we break the ethnic, tribal, and racial barriers. Love will cause us to repay good for evil. It is because of love that we are able to forgive even those who have killed our loved ones. With love, we live our complete faith in exercising our gifts and talents, as Paul wrote in 1 Corinthians 12:31, through "the most excellent way."

## FAVORITISM UNDERMINES OUR FAITH

James goes on to teach us that the follower of Christ must not give undue preference to those who have power, wealth, or position. He asks how we would treat a wealthy person in fancy clothes that came to our church, compared with a poor person in shabby clothes. Who would receive the nicest place to sit? I think I know the answer. When I go visit our churches in Burundi, I am asked to sit in the nicest chairs on the platform. That's not because I'm wealthy, of course, but because of my leadership position in the church. Some of our churches have no chairs or benches. People sit on logs, on stones, on whatever they can find. Or they just sit on the floor. But usually there are a few benches and one of them would probably be offered to the wealthy person.

Of course the teaching here is about much more than where people are seated in church. James is challenging his readers to love others regardless of their position or wealth. He points out that God welcomes the poor into prominent places in His kingdom. If God welcomes them regardless of their means, why shouldn't we? Ironically, the rich, who receive our special attention, are sometimes the very ones who exploit us. James says that favoritism is so contrary to God's law of love that it totally nullifies our efforts to please God.

Outsiders oversimplify our conflicts in Burundi, attributing them to the inability of two ethnic groups to live at peace. So many other issues divide our people. The exploitation of the poor by the rich is not restricted to either ethnic group. The wealthy seek power to protect their riches. Sometimes they use the rhetoric of ethnic distrust to serve their own purposes. How can we continue to show favoritism to those with wealth and power, when we are all equal in God's eyes? Our people, most of whom call themselves Christians, should find a new oneness and equality in Christ, without adopting the world's ways of basing worth on wealth.

## THE WEALTHY MUST NOT OPPRESS

A companion teaching in the book of James calls on the wealthy and powerful to abandon their oppressive ways. James says the precious belongings of the wealthy are rotten, corroded, like physical bodies being eaten away. They have underpaid their workers, they have murdered innocent people. "You have lived on earth in luxury and self-indulgence," says James. (James 5:5) His words echo the many passages in the Old Testament, which call the wealthy oppressors to account, for example:

> Hear this, you who trample the needy and do away with the poor of the land, saying, "When will the New Moon be over that we may sell grain, and the Sabbath be ended that we may market wheat?"—skimping the measure, boosting the price and cheating with dishonest scales, buying the poor with silver and the needy for a pair of sandals, selling even the sweepings with the wheat. (Amos 8:4-6)

One of the sad things about the history of colonialism is that we Africans learned many of the worst behaviors of the European officials. We learned to despise those of lower standing. We learned that wealth and position determine worth. We learned that oppressing the powerless is the privilege of the wealthy. For our country to survive, we must "un-learn" these lessons and learn that all are equal in God's sight.

## WORDS CAN DESTROY OR HEAL

James gave great prominence to a very simple truth, that our words have the potential for great good or evil. He compared the tongue to the bit in a horse's mouth, the rudder of a ship, or the spark that starts a forest fire. James said we praise God with our tongue, that we go to church faithfully, but we use the same tongue to curse people who are created in God's image and are fully loved by God. This makes me think about my country, where so many attend church and call themselves Christians, but speak with such hatred about their enemies.

This passage is very helpful in our personal lives. Who of us has not hurt others with poorly chosen words, words that replaced love with cleverness or harshness, words that destroyed instead of healed. But the teaching applies as well to the words exchanged between our political and ethnic factions. One group makes statements and the other retaliates. Hateful words escalate to hateful actions. As James says, our words are too often "full of deadly poison." (James 3:8)

## WISDOM PRODUCES PEACE

One of the most powerful sections in the book of James describes two contrasting patterns of human conduct. One is false wisdom, evidenced by bitter envy, selfishness, and all sorts of evil behavior. True wisdom, says James, is "pure; then peace-loving, considerate, submissive, full of mercy and good fruit, impartial and sincere." (James 3:17) False wisdom, on the other hand, is evidenced by improper desires and escalates to envy, then to quarreling and fighting, then to murder.

This passage in James includes a beautiful statement about the person with true wisdom: "Peacemakers who sow in peace raise a harvest of righteousness." (3:18) James was writing the passage to people who were very familiar with agriculture. They knew that a well-planted and carefully tended crop would almost always grow and produce the harvest that is desired. In my country as well, the farmer knows that carefully tilled soil, good seed, ample moisture, and plenty of sunshine will result in abundant crops. The wise person, says James, is one who is faithful in God's work, who is pure, considerate, merciful, and impartial. Such a person can count on raising a crop of righteousness. In the Scripture, righteousness is often synonymous with justice, so we see a direct linkage of peace and justice, which is as it should be.

## GOD PROVIDES GRACE WHEN WE SUFFER

The book of James begins and ends with some important teaching on being faithful in the midst of suffering. Near the beginning of the book James writes: "Consider it pure joy, my brothers, whenever you face trials of many kinds, because you know that the testing of your faith develops perseverance. Perseverance must finish its work so that you may be mature and complete, not lacking anything." (1:2-4) Then near the end of the book, James wrote, "As you know, we consider blessed those who have persevered. You have heard of Job's perseverance and have seen what the Lord finally brought about. The Lord is full of compassion and mercy." (5:11)

As I have pointed out in a previous chapter, my family and Felicity's family have been affected by the killings in our country. We are not alone in this. In fact, I doubt if I could find any family in our country that has not lost loved ones. For a time we almost became numb from the constant news of more people killed and injured. Some might have died as a direct result of their faithfulness to Christ. More often it had nothing to do with their faith. They were murdered because of their ethnic identity, because of being better educated than others, or because they were blamed for previous killings.

But God has been gracious to our country in spite of all of the suffering. People faced with the reality of dying at almost any time have been forced to address their own spiritual needs. Consequently, our churches have actually grown during the years of suffering. People have cried out to God amidst the horrible events of these years. They have turned from being "Sunday only" Christians to those who are serious about living for God and, if necessary, willing to die for God. None of us who have lived through these horrible events would want to do so again, but we would testify that God has been very close to us. It may be there are more people who are being faithful to God today than before the events of the last thirty-five years in Burundi.

**David, you said these thoughts are the ones you would present to all the people of our country if you had the chance. You know, in many countries of Africa, speaking to all the people at once would be impossible, short of God performing a miracle. Some countries have dozens of different languages, and no one understands them all. As you've said, Burundi is different. Everyone speaks Kirundi. If we could connect with every home, every school, every business, and every church, it would be possible to speak to everyone at once.**

**That's not going to happen any time soon. But Emmanuel, maybe it will in your generation. Through the Internet and computers, people are now able to communicate with one another tens of thousands of miles apart. Modern technology is reaching us here in Burundi. You've seen the lab with laptop computers at the Great Lakes School of Theology. This kind of technology could be used for evil as well, but I'm optimistic enough to believe it can help us in our problems of conflict and in spreading the Gospel among our people.**

**David, I'm still trying to picture you speaking to everyone in the country at once. Let's say we were able to arrange that. If all our people were to hear that God loves them**

and calls us to love each other, would it make a difference? The Bible talks about beating our swords into plowshares. We don't use swords exactly, but much of the killing has been done with spears and machetes. These and the guns in the country could be put to constructive uses as hoes and shovels, for cultivating our land.

Think about all the wasted manpower in the violence in our country. We could have raised so many crops, we could have built better homes, we could have improved our roads. I'm sure there are undeveloped natural resources, maybe undiscovered mineral wealth, if we could set aside our fighting and join our energies in useful endeavors.

You picked a very good book in the Bible for your imaginary sermon to the nation, David. I have another passage for a follow-up sermon to the people.

What's that Emmanuel?

I was reading the Bible for my devotions this morning, in the book of Ephesians. There's a passage in chapter two that sounds like it was written just for Burundians. I've got my New Testament along. May I read it for you?

Of course, Emmanuel. I know the passage you mean and I love it very much. Go ahead and read it.

"But now in Christ Jesus you who once were far away have been brought near through the blood of Christ. For he himself is our peace, who has made the two one and has destroyed the barrier, the dividing wall of hostility, by abolishing in his flesh the law with its commandments and regulations. His purpose was to create in himself one new man out of the two, thus making peace, and in this one body to reconcile both of them to God through the cross, by which he put to death their hostility. He came and preached peace to you who were far away and peace to those who were near." (Ephesians 2:13-17)

David, do you think it's ever possible that the "two men" spoken of in Ephesians and represented by the two major ethnic groups in our country can ever be one?

Emmanuel, we never were two different people. We have been so badly corrupted by sin and evil that we have begun to believe we are actually two completely different kinds of people and can't ever live in peace together. That's total nonsense. We are one people and always have been. We simply have to believe that we can throw away the false perceptions of differences that can never be reconciled. Sure, we have lots of little individual differences, but we are and have always been one people. I take a lot of hope from the verse at the end of the chapter you were reading, "And in him you too are being built together to become a dwelling in which God lives by his Spirit." The key here is building together and even more important, to invite God's Spirit to come and live with us. We then will stop seeing differences and realize we are all one.

"Reconciliation is not merely 'feeling good' but doing what is right. Besides, reconciliation does not occur between 'whites' and 'non-whites,' or between ruler and ruled. Genuine reconciliation does not occur between oppressor and oppressed, it occurs between persons, persons who face each other in their authentic, vulnerable, and yet hopeful humanity. And therefore liberation... is inevitably bound up with reconciliation. And forgiveness."

–Allan Boesak

# 9

# WORKING FOR PEACE AND JUSTICE

Our work for peace in Burundi has taken a number of forms. Because of the urgency of ministering to physical needs after the killings in 1993, we formed three crisis committees, one for each of the quarterly meetings in Burundi Yearly Meeting. The superintendents of the quarterly meetings served as the chairmen of the committees. We distributed rice and beans to the displaced people in the camps and the dispersed people, those not in camps but hiding away from their homes. Many people felt it was far too dangerous to work out in their fields, so there were no crops being planted and there was very little food.

By the latter part of 1994, we wanted to expand our work beyond the people associated with the Friends churches, so we formed a peace committee, open to people of all faiths. The staff of the Friends hospital at Kibimba took the lead in forming the committee, since it was widely known that the hospital had accepted patients from all ethnic groups and was not identified with either group. Some of those from the camps of displaced persons were included on the peace committee. One of those on the committee was a person who escaped a burning building and was still trying to cope with the trauma of his near-death experience. We worked closely with the commander of the local camp for displaced persons to obtain information about the numbers of people needing food. One might think of such a person as the "enemy," but it was our experience that the commander was a reasonable and fair human being, not a person with an agenda of revenge and hatred.

In 1996, my wife and I decided to leave Burundi for a while, after hearing that I was on a death list drawn up by some Tutsi extremists. Those on the list were Hutu people with education and with leadership positions. This was a very painful decision. I did not want to leave, since I knew that it was going to be difficult to stay active with peacemaking work and with church leadership while living in another country. My wife, Felicity, and I prayed about this and felt that it was time to go, for safety purposes and so that we might have a much-needed vacation. We left Burundi on May 25, 1996, encountering no difficulty in leaving the country.

Some might have considered our departure from Burundi to be cowardly, but we were not obsessed with fear. Deep in my heart I had a conviction that my life had been spared during the killings of our pastoral students at Kwibuka and I still felt that God must have more work for me to do. Going to Kenya was a way of increasing the chances of continuing that work later.

I used some of the time in Nairobi to translate peace materials into Kirundi. I completed the translation of *Peace and Reconciliation as a Paradigm* by Hizkias Assefa, and finished the translation of another book, *Peace and Democracy*. I also obtained permission to translate a peace manual developed in Liberia, *KOUKATON*, for teaching peace to children.

In doing this translation work, I was mindful of the importance of the Kirundi-Kinyarwanda language. This language is one of the most widely-spoken languages in Sub-Saharan Africa, after Kiswahili. People in Rwanda speak Kinyarwanda, while in Burundi it is Kirundi. In the eastern part of the Democratic Republic of Congo many people use either Kirundi or Kinyarwanda, along with their local languages. I have heard people in Western Tanzania speak what sounded like a variation of Kirundi-Kinyarwanda. They do not want to call it Kirundi because they are not Burundians nor Kinyarwanda because they are not Rwandans, so they call the language Giha. I have been told that people in

Northwest Uganda also use Kinyarwanda as one of the major Ugandan languages.

I have coined a name, *"uruyaga,"* for this language spoken by 22 million people. The name is based on the fact that the language is spoken in the region of the Great Lakes (*Ibiyaga Binini*), and from the root word *"Kuyaga,"* meaning to communicate. Part of the point of giving a new name to this widely used language is to call attention to its potential for helping the people who use the language to learn to live peacefully with one another. Some have said that the reason Tanzania has not had ethnic violence is because of the unifying influence of the Kiswahili language, which is used throughout the country and among the many tribes. During Mwalimu Julius Nyerere's early regime, he declared Kiswahili to be the official national language, helping to strengthen the feeling of being one people.

Because of the vast number of people who speak uruyaga, I believe that peace materials can have a great impact in the region. That is why I chose to translate peace materials into Kirundi instead of French. Even though French has been used in the secondary schools in Burundi, Rwanda, and Congo, there are actually very few in the region who can easily read French. A census taken in Burundi in 1991 showed that there were 6 million people in all, of whom only 3 million had attended some sort of school. Those who had been able to go beyond the primary school were no more than 150,000.

Another benefit of my time in Kenya was the opportunity to connect with the outside world and create more awareness of the need for peace in Burundi. I wanted a chance to let people in other countries know that the problems of one country are the problems of all countries. I wanted to raise the awareness of as many people as possible so that they might feel more concerned about the violence in our region. I wanted more people to grasp the impact of violence on the lives of Burundi's children, men, women, and elderly, regardless of his/her ethnic identity. I wanted those who knew how to pray, to pray. I wanted those with international authority, whether religious, political, or humanitarian to use their influence to encourage Burundians to find a peaceful solution to the crisis.

One of the ways I was able to meet and speak to numerous people was during a tour in the United States organized by the American Friends Service Committee in 1996. Over a period of about six weeks I was able to travel to 22 cities in 19 states, to give 66 media interviews, including seven meetings with newspaper editorial boards. I made 21 presentations to seminary, college, and high school audiences, 15 churches (worship services), and 39 community groups. Among those visits I will highlight two important meetings.

The Washington, D.C., segment of the tour was designed to provide direct contact with people at the highest level of U.S. policy-making. At the State Department, I met with Ambassador Richard Bogosian, former U.S. ambassador to Burundi, who was then posted at the State Department as special coordinator on Rwanda/Burundi, and Alex Laskaris, Burundi desk officer. Howard Wolpe, President Clinton's special representative for Rwanda/Burundi, was scheduled to attend, but was ill that day. As I described my experiences to the State Department officials, they were attentive and sympathetic. Ambassador Bogosian said that U.S. policy was principally aimed at bringing about peace in Burundi, as well as reform and social progress.

The staff of the Quaker United Nations Office coordinated an informal, off-the-record luncheon for diplomats and members of the U.N. Secretariat on the subject of directions of peace making in Burundi. The Quaker House was filled almost to capacity with 19 guests (24 personal invitations were sent) including the ambassador of Tanzania, Daudi Ngelautwa Mwakawago, three representatives from the Security Council (Mission of Chile, Botswana, and Republic of Korea), and other diplomats and non-government organization representatives. In my brief presentation, I stressed the need for the international community to become far more involved with the conflicts in Burundi and Rwanda.

In addition to these many meetings and gatherings in the United States, I was also able to visit England, Germany, and Sweden. I was encouraged by the many who expressed interest and concern about the situation in Burundi.

Before our departure from Burundi, we had established what we called a House of Peace in the town of Gitega. It was an effort to help sensitize the youth and expose them to various alternatives to violence. With the help of the Mennonite Central Committee, we brought in a great number of peace materials—books, news magazines, newspapers, and leaflets—and made them available to the public to read. The Mennonite Central Committee had provided us with a team of young volunteers we called the peace volunteers. They worked with our youth and women in different projects, and helped us distribute relief to the needy people. Some of them even spoke in our peace workshops.

The Friends Church was the first religious denomination to organize peace seminars and workshops in the country. In one of our first peace seminars, I remember we were reflecting on the role of women in the violence in our country. To our amazement, the participants told us that some women were actively involved in the violence. They had not only failed to admonish their children against participating in the violence, but had provided a terrible example of anger and hatred in front of their children by their own actions.

During these peace efforts, we sent one of our members to the "Responding to Conflict" training at the Quaker Study Center at Woodbrooke, England. When he returned, he trained men and women from the Catholic and Protestant churches and from both ethnic groups on constructive methods of dealing with conflicts. Upon completing the training we helped the participants organize a group that is continuing to conduct conflict resolution workshops throughout the country. This project is today known as the "Ministry of Peace and Reconciliation under the Cross" (MiParec).

Because I had been convinced that God had spared my life so that I might contribute to peace building, I got involved in a variety of activities to promote nonviolence and with initiatives that would help people change their violent way of life. I wanted people to work toward the reestablishment of peaceful behavior, tolerance, acceptance of one another, and particularly forgiveness and reconciliation. But it was not easy to put my vision into practice while living in Kenya.

During this time, a friend of mine, David Ndaruhutse, the founder of the African Revival Ministry, died in an airplane crash in the hills in eastern Congo. He was going to a gospel crusade with other pastors. The news about his death was devastating to all of us who knew him, for we loved and appreciated him very much. While in Nairobi, I found it very helpful to go to the Nairobi arboretum for prayer and meditation. After David Ndaruhutse's death, I was at the arboretum and felt that God was speaking to me just as He spoke to Joshua: "Moses my servant is dead. Now then,…get ready to cross…." The passage speaks about crossing to the land of Canaan, but the impression that God gave me was that it was time for me to return to Burundi. I went home and told my wife about my leading from God and we immediately made arrangements to go back. It was in May 1998, that we were able to return.

Looking back on this decision to return to Burundi, it is clear that it made possible renewed and expanded efforts toward reconciliation. Among the initiatives that were launched at this time:

• The establishment of the Peace Primary School in Gitega, in which children are exposed to the values of peaceful interaction from an early age.

• The founding of the Great Lakes School of Theology in Bujumbura, in which men and women from the region are being trained on issues of leadership and how to cope with the challenges of the region.

• The signing of the agreement between the Friends Church and the government of Burundi on the partnership in education.

• The continuation of the Kibimba Peace Committee and other projects aimed at the healing of the trauma among the population.

These efforts and others have as their goal the adoption of a new ethic of love and a new way of caring for other people.

## SEEKING JUSTICE AND SPARING A LIFE

There have been many innocent victims of the violence of the past three decades, but fortunately there have been a few cases of the innocent being spared. When the violence flared up again in 1993, Samson Gahungu was the Burundi Yearly Meeting presiding clerk and was also one of the staff members at the Kibimba high school. When the trouble started, the staff had to close the school. The classrooms, dining hall, dormitories, and library became home to 3,000 displaced people and all their belongings, including their cows, goats, and chickens. The Friends Church at Kibimba, which could contain 1,500 people, could no longer be used for worship, because the displaced people occupied it as well. Samson and most of the other residents at Kibimba fled and spent time in the valleys, because of the dangers of the military operations in the area.

At the 1995 General Assembly of the Burundi National Council of Churches, the Friends delegates advocated the establishment of a department to give leadership to the crisis responses. As one of the Friends delegates, I argued that it was not acceptable that an organization responsible for activities related to the spiritual life of our people would sit back and helplessly watch the tragic events in the country. After a lengthy explanation of why it was important to have such a department, the members of the General Assembly asked if I could think of a person who could come to work in the department. I suggested Samson Gahungu and his name was immediately accepted. The organization was named the Department of Peace, Reconciliation and Evangelism. There was no money for the department, but we encouraged Samson to trust that God would provide the funds for this work. It was not long after he got there that donors gave sufficient funds to start the program, buy a vehicle, a computer, a photocopy machine, a telephone, furniture, and other office materials.

Samson had barely got the office established and the program under way when on February 15, 1996, police officers came to Samson's office, arrested him and took him to jail. The police charged him with participating in a particularly terrible killing of a number of Kibimba High School students. The students were seized by an angry group of villagers, were dragged to a petrol station, and were set on fire. To this day, I find it terribly hard to believe that there were those who could have thought Samson had a part in this tragedy. He is one of the most gentle and godly leaders of the Friends Church in Burundi. One can only speculate that those who implicated him in the killing were envious of the position he held at the high school.

The policemen treated him roughly, squeezed him into their small car, and verbally abused him. Samson prayed that God would forgive his false accusers and also prayed that God would protect him in whatever ill treatment he might receive in prison.

Samson wrote to me from prison:

To me prison is stagnation, handcuffed in a cell; crouching in a tiny space, behind walls and bars where you can only see the sky; seeing everything from one half-lit unventilated room enclosed on six sides—fortified walls, roof and floor smoke-blackened and filth-stained; deprivation of family and friends; stream of endless thoughts, monotony, worry, discouragement, loneliness, sickness, hunger, thirst, and discomfort....

Yet despite all this and more, my heart is truly free because Jesus is my faithful and unfailing friend. When I was arrested on 15 February I asked God for courage to accept his will. At the same time I forgave all those responsible for my unjust arrest because, as Jesus said, "they know not what they do." I head the department of peace and reconciliation at the Burundi National Council of Churches, so not to have been able to forgive would have made prison a humiliation! 1 Corinthians 10:13 gives me daily comfort: I know that I will not be tested beyond my strength and by this comes my daily survival. Several weeks ago, some prisoners stole many clothes by pulling them through the holes in a storage room. They sold them to other prisoners at very low prices (less than 1 cent). I was in need of clothing and was tempted to buy a piece, just as anybody else was buying them, but I realized that if I bought the clothing, I would be encouraging the thieves to steal more. I remembered also that the clothing and shoes of those who trust in the Lord can last up to 40 years like the Israelites in the wilderness because of God's grace (Deuteronomy 8:4; 29:4).

Every morning at about 4:00 a.m., Samson would wake up and pray, especially for his pending court case. One day as he was praying he heard a voice call out a Scripture reference: Luke 4:38. He did not know the verse, but because it was four days until he was to appear in court he thought that God was giving him words of encouragement such as *"do not be afraid"* or *"I will be with you."* He memorized the reference from Luke so he could look it up in the morning. As soon as there was light in his cell he opened his Bible and read the passage, but he was disappointed because the passage did not include words of assurance as he had expected. The passage says, "Jesus left the synagogue and went to the home of Simon. Now Simon's mother-in-law was suffering from a high fever, and they asked Jesus to help her. So he bent over her and rebuked the fever, and it left her. She got up at once and began to wait on them." This passage was not what he had expected at all.

Samson then asked a fellow prisoner who was also a Christian to help him interpret the passage. After reading the passage the other prisoner was so happy and said to Samson, "How could you be so ignorant as to not realize that the fever that is talked about in the passage is like the heat of your court case?" The man added that "just as people asked Jesus to help Simon's mother-in-law, so are many people, all over the world, praying for you." He assured Samson that he was going to be acquitted and released, because his "high fever" was over, thanks to the fact that God had heard the prayers of many people on his behalf. Samson accepted this interpretation and thanked God for granting him release from prison, even though it hadn't happened yet.

Samson had two preliminary hearings prior to his trial on September 30, 1997. On April 25, 1997, he was accused of having been responsible for actions leading to the massacre of October 1993. Were he to be found guilty, such action would be punishable by death, according to the Penal Code. During the hearing he was accompanied by two lawyers, a Malian visiting "co-operant" and Maitre Gahungu Raphael, whom Samson described as "sincere and very ready to defend him." Maitre Gahungu is from the Tutsi ethnic group. During the first hearing the judges had somehow concluded that Samson's case was related to that of Firmat, the former director of the Kibimba High School. In that case, Firmat had been sentenced to death in connection with the Kibimba massacre. But it was quickly pointed out that Samson's name did not appear in the records of the Firmat case and he had taken no part in it. Samson's lawyer argued that he should be released immediately, but the judges asked for a written request and scheduled a second hearing.

The second hearing was held on May 9, 1997. After the departure of the Malian lawyer, some of the documents were not handed over to Maitre Gahungu, and a third hearing was requested. The third hearing took place on September 30, 1997, at the Chambre Criminelle in Bujumbura. At this hearing, Maitre Gahungu and Samson decided to change their approach. Instead of asking for unconditional release, Gahungu requested that Samson's case go before the Tribunal, in an effort to clear Samson's name once and for all. Two separate trials were scheduled for September 30 and the small courtroom was packed. I was one of those who stood in the back of the room for the whole hearing. Many of those present were friends and well-wishers of Samson's, although he also saw some of those who had accused him. Unlike the trial of Firmat, the atmosphere was very calm and respectful. The judges finally went into deliberation at 4:00 p.m. and delivered the verdict at 7:30 p.m. Samson was acquitted after 595 days of incarceration and was released from prison the next day.

Samson was acquitted because, according to the presiding judge, the accusations made by the prosecutor were without foundation. The prosecutor blamed Samson for being a leader in the violence. Said the prosecutor, "He had to be, because he was the only intellectual present at the time and the villagers could not have organized this alone." He argued that if Samson had not collaborated with them he would have been in danger and would have had to flee. Five witnesses for the prosecutor (all of them former students of Kibimba) didn't appear at the trial despite numerous previous appearances and the sixth witness, the assistant director from the Kibimba school, was a witness both for and against Samson. This man testified that while he didn't see anything, he had heard it said that Samson had taken a motorcycle and was going back and forth between the site of the killings and the school, organizing the massacre. The witnesses accused Samson of detaining students in a classroom in order to facilitate their round-up and massacre.

Samson's witnesses, on the other hand, testified that they saw villagers come to the school and say they were going to keep the students captive until their president was released.

According to these witnesses, the villagers threatened Samson, but Samson hid some of the students and negotiated for the release of others. Many of the students were wounded and Samson managed to convince the villagers to allow the stronger ones to carry the wounded ones to the hospital. He asked for 8 to 12 students for each sick one, and thereby managed to get about half of the group to safety. At this time, Samson did not believe that the villagers intended to kill the remaining students, but were just going to tie them up and humiliate them. He then went to the hospital to check on the wounded students. One of Samson's witnesses was a survivor of the massacre. He went into a detailed account of what happened at the site of the massacre and how he escaped.

In Samson's defense, his lawyer made several references to a book, *Genocide d'Octobre 1993,* pointing out that Samson's name did not appear in the list of people accused of complicity in the Kibimba massacres. Some are still in prison waiting for a hearing. As in so many prisons in Africa where the state lacks enough financial resources, conditions are not easy. Prisoners receive one meal per day, usually some beans and cassava bread. Samson, however, was in good physical condition throughout most of his detention and was never physically abused. He was allowed to receive visitors and was especially thankful to see them, including many American friends. Finally, Samson was acquitted and released on October 1, 1997. We, who had prayed with Samson and had done what we could to gain his release, joined him in giving praise and glory to God for this wonderful answer to prayer.

**David, that's a wonderful story of God's deliverance. I think you said you also felt a special hand of protection and deliverance on the way back from the Ruhororo refugee camp. I'd like to hear about that.**

During the crisis in 1993 I had heard that the members of the Friends church in Mubuga had helped each other during the killings and I decided to go there to encourage them and commend them for their brave actions. Moses (my driver) and I drove our van to the area on a Sunday morning. On the way to Mubuga Friends Church, one has to go through what is called an "Internally Displaced People's Camp." There is always a road-block manned by at least three soldiers in such places and during the crisis going through it was always tense and dangerous. Our destination was about two miles from the camp and there were some of our members in the camp to whom we gave a lift, as our van could take up to 15 passengers.

We had a very good service at the Mubuga church. I shared the word of God, mostly about how love and forgiveness work together and how those qualities are ways of putting one's faith in action. I commended the church members for their brave actions in expressing love for each other, even when everyone else was hating his/her neighbors and when others were killing each other.

From the people at Mubuga Friends Church, I learned that during the most difficult times of the crisis when the Hutus were killing Tutsis, the Hutu members of the church had hidden Tutsi people from those who wanted to kill them. A few days later when the Tutsis were killing Hutus, the Tutsi members hid the Hutus. I was so overjoyed about the brave actions of the church people that during the worship service when they sang choruses, I danced and rejoiced and gave praise to the Lord. I thanked God for using these brave people to show the rest of us that He is still on the throne, even when people think that things are out of His control.

On the way back, I could not help but think about the coura-geous and loving people at Mubuga Friends and what it meant to act like that and how it could have cost them their lives. I remem-bered stories I had read about Germans hiding Jews and how many times they were arrested along with the "enemies." While thinking about these wonderful people I saw that we had arrived back at the camp's roadblock. It was about 3:00 p.m., which is a typical time for worship services to be finished in Burundi.

At the camp's roadblock I noticed there were no soldiers anywhere in sight. In fact, there was no one around at all! The roadblock actually consisted of a long thin eucalyptus log placed on top of two short posts. Moses and I began to worry, since it was starting to get dark. We both had heard about people being killed at this very spot. Moses suggested that we go around the roadblock and continue on our way, since there was space for our vehicle to pass and there was nobody to open the barrier. I finally agreed, but just as we had managed to maneuver the vehicle around the barrier and back on the road, a soldier came and stopped us. He was so furious that we could see the anger all over his face. Even before he asked to see our papers, he insulted us and spit towards us. He was full of hatred and rage. He took our identification papers, vehicle papers, and told us to wait for him. We knew we were in serious trouble, based on stories from other such situations. I was so afraid. We begged for the soldier's forgiveness, but he felt no mercy for us. He told us that we should not pray to him because he was not our god.

Meanwhile, the crowd had gathered around our vehicle and I heard two men telling the soldiers that we had just passed through the camp some while ago from the other direction without stopping, which of course was not true. This made the soldier even angrier and he began accusing us of crimes we had never committed. At this point we did not say anything. We did not know what else we could do.

As we were waiting for the soldier to return, another soldier came. I still remember his face. He looked different from the others. Surprisingly, he did not have a gun. He started pleading with the other solders on our behalf. I saw him talking to a soldier, following him around like a street child begging for a piece of bread. Finally, the first soldier came up to us, handed the van keys to Moses, and told him to reverse the vehicle and drive as if we were just arriving at the roadblock. As Moses was turning the vehicle around, I was wondering what would happen next. I was ready to lift the whole vehicle over the roadblock if that was what the soldier wanted. When we approached the roadblock, the first soldier lifted it for us to go through. We stopped on the other side and he handed us back our papers, telling us never to bypass a roadblock again. We didn't see the second soldier again while this was happening. It seemed to us that this soldier was an angel God had sent to deliver us from death. On the way back home, we thanked God for His wonderful deliverance from danger.

"To be forgiven is to feel the weight of the past lifted from our shoulders, to feel the stain of past wrong-doing washed away. To be forgiven is to feel free to step into the future unburdened by the precedent of who we have been and what we have done in previous times."

—Harold S. Kushner

# 10

# THE WAY FORWARD THROUGH FORGIVENESS

Peace will come when there is a change of mentality, when Burundians no longer just see the ethnic differences, but see people as human beings created in the image of God, deserving respect and the right to live. There is a Quaker expression that "there is that of God in every human being," including those who are thought of as our enemies. This is a complete change of thinking from the "eye for an eye" approach, which prevails in many parts of the world, including Burundi.

There was a consultation of Hutu and Tutsi church leaders in Nairobi in February 1996, dealing with the role the church could play in restoring peace. One of the statements developed at the consultation was as follows:

> Our vision and dream for Burundi is that it should be a country living in peace, justice, unity and with security for all. We dream of a land where everyone agrees to live by the Rule of Law as it is only by such an agreement that Law and Order may prevail. We also see democratic, stable, and prosperous Burundi offering equal rights, equal educational and equal job opportunities for all.

This dream brings to mind a Scripture verse that says, "where there is no vision, the people perish." (Proverbs 29:18 KJV)

In developing a vision for a better future for Burundi, different churches have been doing it in their different ways. Of course the question is whether or not the churches are doing enough. While I am not saying the Friends churches are doing better than anyone else, our people have made some significant progress in planting the seeds of peace. We have been translating peace and conflict resolution materials into Kirundi in an effort to help people change their mentality. We have been preaching God's love that is able to change people and make them see things differently and cause them to forgive. We have been seeking to demonstrate that forgiveness is a strong weapon for stopping the vicious cycle of violence. This is our challenge to all Burundians, particularly Christians.

In my opinion, the major cause of conflict in Burundi is the struggle for power. Will the people who call themselves the *"incabwenge"* (the intellectuals) be the only ones with significant power in our country? I have observed that the powerful ones want to remain where they are at all cost, but the discontented ones want to increase their power, which often means higher privileges and higher salaries. There have been successive strikes in Burundi, which in my opinion are due to this power struggle. It is said that sometimes these strikes were organized in a period when the government was demanding an *"effort de guerre"* (war sacrifice) from every citizen, to be able to cope with the crisis.

While this book has not focused primarily on politics, I want to express my opinion that we have established too many political parties in Burundi. Ours is a country in which people are not used to freely expressing their views on governance. For this reason, the creation of too many political parties in which the leaders' views are not yet fully considered, is simply a way for a few leaders of those parties to gain power. A political party leader's followers, as I have observed, empower him or her and he or she expects them to accept directives. whether for good or bad. We saw that in the crisis of 1993—a political leader just said it and the followers just did it!

There is a proverb in Kirundi that says, "a stone that is seen cannot destroy a farmer's hoe" (*Ibuye riserutse ntiriba ricishe isuka*). The proverb means that Burundians should learn to share things in the open. Often people, even Christians, speak evil about others when they are in their sitting rooms with their own people. I once heard of a man who threw his keys at a television screen because it was showing the picture of a person he hated! Hatred must be brought out into the open and dealt with. It is imperative to expose what troubles the community. Through dialogue people develop more positive feelings about one another. During the crisis, especially in the Bujumbura suburbs, people have killed each other with the excuse that "if I do not kill him first, he might kill me." In dialogue, people are supposed to make agreements. It is a process of giving and receiving, not of demanding and taking. This is exactly what the traditional leaders were able to do in their mediation processes. This is why I think it is a good idea to restore the role of the traditional leaders, which in the past has played a major part in settling tensions and in rehabilitating crucial values such as respect for all human beings.

Another challenge is to learn how to deal appropriately with land and property disputes. In Burundi most of the court cases have dealt with disagreements over land. When land ownership issues are mismanaged, there are conflicts, even between a father and a son, or a brother and brother. If this is the case for family members, how much more so among those who are not related? I have heard more than one person say that part of the reason President Melchior Ndadaye was killed was because of the way land issues were handled. The Hutu refugees who had fled the 1972 killings started to return to their home areas in southern Burundi after the FRODEBU's victory, but this created huge disputes over land ownership. There were arguments over who first owned the land and property and how it was acquired. I know that in other parts of Africa there are problems between the sedentary and nomadic people over access to the land. It is important to settle the refugee issues because they are connected with land and property disputes. All refugees dream of a time when they will be able to return home, as this Sudanese lamented in a refugee camp in Kenya:

Away from your homeland
anyone can treat you as if you're worthless

Away from your homeland
you endure life as a vagrant

Away from your homeland
you meet prejudice and misunderstanding

Away from your homeland your integrity is ruined

Away from your homeland people see you as useless

Away from your homeland your kinfolk faints away,
the respected elder as well as the child

Away from your homeland
you persevere amidst disaster

Away from your homeland
you're like a baby that's been weaned too soon

Away from your homeland
you're disowned by friends

Away from your homeland
you're devoured by a toothless animal

Away from your homeland
you're made into a docile creature

Away from your homeland
your soul knows deep sorrows

Away from your homeland
life seems useless, useless, useless, too useless.

—Home is Home, Bush is Bush, *Tam-Tam* Volume 11, 1996

There are Burundi refugees in many countries of the world. Christians have a great opportunity to exercise love, caring, and understanding in helping the refugees return and resettle. Along with the material needs of the refugees, love is what they are lacking the most, as the above poem expresses.

There is another poem that connects with a point I want to make. I have written this book for Burundians and non-Burundians alike. Outsiders, no matter how skilled and concerned they may be, cannot solve our problems for us. The conflicts involve Burundians and it is the Burundians who must set about to solve them effectively. But that is no excuse for the rest of the world to ignore us. Non-Burundians are called by God to pray with us in finding solutions, to give appropriate support to reconciliation efforts, and especially to abstain from helping those who seek to undermine our work for peace. There was a Brethren in Christ relief worker in Burundi in the early sixties who wrote a book and in its conclusion challenged other non-Burundians to be faithful to the teaching of the Good Samaritan:

Two donkey hours away
From Zion city lay
A beaten man.
Levite and Priest espied
And heard the man who cried,
But passed him by.
A few jet hours away
From San Francisco lay
More sore-beat men.
We fly too high to hear
The cry and see the tear—
We eat our lunch.

(Wingert, p. 108)

In the final analysis, only forgiveness will heal the wounds and stop the violence. Those of us who believe in God know that when we have peace in our hearts and are reconciled with

God and with ourselves, peace will overflow to our neighbors and even to the rest of God's creation. Peace is possible for Burundi and there are advocates for it, Hutu and Tutsi alike. We must enter into the process of forgiveness and begin to love one another. Many of us believe that the weapons of war should be turned into plough shares and pruning hooks, as it says in the book of Isaiah. We are in this together, we should support and uphold each other and never give up.

> **David, how can I thank you for these times we have spent together? You have given me much to think about. I cannot be the same person after what you have taught me. What can I do to repay you?**

> **Well, Emmanuel, of course I would never expect a payment in a literal sense, but there is something you can do that would make me very happy. I want to share a vision with you that the Lord has given me for the people of Burundi. All I ask is that you pass it along to people whenever you get the chance.**

The vision begins with seeing a community of people who, individually and decisively, humble themselves and acknowledge that they have lived a life of faith with little works, if any. In local churches in various parts of the country, in pastors', leaders', and women's retreats, during the youth camps and other gatherings of all kinds, people must be summoned and encouraged to live the Christian life in a practical way. They must understand the Scripture passage in James 2:17 that faith without works is dead. They must also come to believe there is hope, that faith can be healed/resurrected when one lives a life that impacts others positively.

It must become clear to our people that the reason there has been so much violence in this so-called Christian country is that Christians have not extended the love of God from their hearts to their neighbors, those of different backgrounds, and even to their enemies. People must take up the challenge to live actively as Christians and put an end to the hatred that is based on being from different ethnic groups. Interviews on the Burundi Christian Radio as well as the National Radio, teachings about God in schools and other institutions must focus on the integration of faith and loving actions. People must seek to impact each other by applying the Christian principles of peace, love, reconciliation, justice, and forgiveness. Then and only then can we begin unlocking the horns in Burundi.

CPSIA information can be obtained
at www.ICGtesting.com
Printed in the USA
FFOW03n0001290318
46017011-46915FF